Visitors to Monticello

VISITORS TO

MONTICELLO

EDITED BY

MERRILL D. PETERSON

UNIVERSITY PRESS OF VIRGINIA

Charlottesville

THE UNIVERSITY PRESS OF VIRGINIA
Copyright © 1989 by the Rector and Visitors
of the University of Virginia

First published 1989

Frontispiece: The Sage of Monticello. Portrait by Thomas Sully,
1821–22. Courtesy of the West Point Museum Collections,
United States Military Academy, West Point, N.Y.

Library of Congress Cataloging-in-Publication Data
Visitors to Monticello / edited by Merrill D. Peterson.
    p.   cm.
    Includes bibliographical references.
    ISBN 0-8139-1231-8.—ISBN 0-8139-1232-6 (pbk.)
    1. Monticello (Va.) 2. Jefferson, Thomas, 1743–1826—Homes and
haunts—Virginia—Albemarle County. I. Peterson, Merrill D.
E332.74.V57   1989
975.5'482—dc20   89-5778
                                         CIP

Printed in the United States of America

CONTENTS

V

CONTENTS

Contents

ILLUSTRATIONS

⚜ PREFACE ⚜

In editing the selections for this volume I have not thought it necessary to expose every myth, reprove every prejudice, or correct every error, nor have I attempted to identify every person and place mentioned in the text. The editing, in sum, has been held to a minimum required for general understanding. A certain amount of repetition is unavoidable in the visitors' accounts, because all are descriptive of Monticello. I have tried to limit repetition by the judicious choice of texts as well as by occasional omissions indicated by ellipses.

I wish to acknowledge the assistance, directly or indirectly, of James A. Bear, Jr., for his research on the history of Monticello; Daniel P. Jordan, Executive Director of the Thomas Jefferson Memorial Foundation, and members of his staff, especially Lucia C. Stanton, Director of Research; Michael F. Plunkett, Curator of Manuscripts, and William H. Runge, Curator of the McGregor Collection, University of Virginia Library; and to Gail A. Moore and the proficient staff of the Word Processing Center of the Faculty of Arts and Sciences in the University.

Visitors to Monticello

$\int$

∽ Introduction ⟫

MONTICELLO, the historic home of Thomas Jefferson, has been welcoming visitors for more than two hundred years. Even during Jefferson's lifetime it acquired the character of a monument, a museum, and a shrine to which foreigners as well as American citizens—the ordinary with the rich and famous, admirers with detractors—beat a path. At the master's death Monticello fell to ruin and decay; but it remained always a fixture of American consciousness, and it rose again, restored and resplendent on its glorious summit, in the twentieth century. Today's visitor is one of an annual procession of 600,000. Indeed, a visit to Monticello has become virtually a patriotic rite for Americans and, for foreign travelers, a mandatory stop on the American grand tour.

A number of the visitors from generation to generation recorded their impressions of Monticello and its creator. It is from this body of writings, various in form, content, and style, that the selections in the present volume are taken. Included are diary entries, personal letters, and memoranda, together with accounts contained in travel books, in recollections and memoirs, in magazine and newspaper articles. Some of the writings are touched with eloquence; some are valuable for the information and observation they provide; all contribute to our understanding of Jefferson and Monticello. In the modern image one is inseparable from the other. President Franklin D. Roosevelt—a frequent visitor—remarked strikingly in 1936: "More than any historic home in America, Monticello appeals to me as an expression of the personality of its builder. In the design, not of the whole alone, but of every room, of every part of every room, in the very furnishings which Jefferson devised on his own drawing board and made in his own workshop, there speaks ready capacity for detail and, above all, creative genius." Today's visitor may have his encounter with that genius extended and enhanced by placing himself imaginatively in the long train of thoughtful journeyers who have gone before him.

Jefferson was a young man, just entering upon the public stage, when he began to build his house on the "little mountain" where he had romped as a boy and which he named in Italian fashion Monticello. He was his own architect, inspired primarily by the great Renaissance master Andrea Palladio, who had returned to Roman antiquity for his models. The house was still uninhabitable in 1772 when Jefferson brought his bride, Martha Wayles Skelton Jefferson, to his bachelor quarters in a small outbuilding on the mountain. They moved in two years later, but another eight years passed before the house was finished. In a sense it was never finished, for Monticello was but the flickering shadow of Jefferson's own shifting and changing mind. Besides, as he once remarked, "architecture is my delight, and putting up and pulling down, one of my favorite amusements." The first Monticello was much smaller than the one the world knows, and it featured, at least in the plan, two-storied porticoes at front and rear. In this house Jefferson's children were born and his wife died. From this house he was driven by Tarleton's dragoons only days after his term as Virginia's governor ended. To this house he welcomed the first notable foreign visitor, the chevalier de Chastellux, to record his impressions in some detail.

Jefferson went to France in 1784 and within a year succeeded Benjamin Franklin as United States minister to the court of Louis XVI. Returning home in the fall of 1789, he was named secretary of state in the new government under the Constitution—a post from which he retired four years later. All the while Monticello was in the care of overseers; even when on duty in New York and Philadelphia, Jefferson spent little time there. But Monticello was never absent from his mind. He made elaborate plans for improvements and upon his retirement in 1794 attempted to carry them out. Priority was given to agricultural improvements on the several farms clustered around Monticello, all worked by black slaves. A nailery was added to Jefferson's small-scale manufactures. In those days Mulberry Row, on the south slope, belched smoke and resounded to the clang of hammers. In 1796 Jefferson began rebuilding the mansion. He wanted more room. His elder daughter, Martha, and her husband, Thomas Mann Randolph, already had four children, with eight more to come; Mary, the younger daughter, would wed John Wayles Eppes in 1797. Like the biblical patriarch, Jefferson wanted his children and grandchildren around him. If that were not sufficient reason, he wished his house to reflect the taste and incorporate the conveniences of the neoclassical buildings he had so much admired in Paris. As the duc de La Rochefoucauld-Liancourt observed, Jefferson had previously studied architecture "in books only"; in Paris, however, he had had the finest models before him and sought now to emulate them. The new plan eliminated the central second story of the original, doubled the width of the house, remounted the east portico, and—the crowning touch—raised a dome above the west portico. Clinging graciously to the summit, the house had a deceptively small appearance. For behind its low symmetrical facade were a mezzanine floor and a skylighted attic floor, which added nine bedrooms for family and guests.

The new Monticello, including the L-shaped terraced wings of his original conception, was finished, or nearly so, when Jefferson retired from the presidency in 1809. Increasingly he turned his thoughts to the grounds and gardens, nothing so elaborate as the English-style landscape gardens he had once envisioned, but flower and vegetable gardens on an ample scale. "I remember well," one of his granddaughters recalled, "when he first returned to Monticello, how immediately he began to prepare new beds for his flowers." An improved vegetable garden, too, was laid out in three long tiers on the sunny slope of the mountain. Within a few years Jefferson focused his passion for building on the last of his creations, the University of Virginia.

Monticello was overrun with visitors during these years, especially after the return of peace in 1815. In the summer months flocks of tourists came up from the low country, perhaps bound for the medicinal springs west of the Blue Ridge. Many stayed overnight. Monticello became a kind of tavern. Martha recalled feeding and putting up as many as fifty guests at a time. Jefferson never complained, but guarded his privacy as best he could and two or three times a year escaped to Poplar Forest, his plantation south of the James River. Everybody came to see the renowned Sage of Monticello. Very few, of course, left any record of their visit. Of those who did, it is obvious that they were more attracted to Jefferson than to his house. The accounts they wrote are especially revealing of the master's appearance, habits, tastes, and conversation. Many thought Monticello whimsical and visionary—perhaps in that respect an accurate reflection of its creator. Whatever their opinion of the house itself, almost everyone agreed that its setting was magnificent, offering the spectator a panorama of mountains, valleys, and forests in which, as William Wirt said, "you see and feel at once, that nothing mean or little could live." It uplifted Jefferson. That alone may explain why he defied reason and precedent to rear his mansion on a densely wooded summit facing the western wilderness. The spectacle long continued to astonish visitors to Monticello.

Jefferson was deeply in debt when he died in 1826. Several months before he had obtained permission from the state to dispose of most of his property by lottery, thereby saving Monticello for his family. The lottery was launched, then suddenly suspended when it appeared that an outpouring of voluntary donations would meet the need. Alas, Jefferson was not cold in his grave before this illusion vanished. Everything was lost. Monticello, as well as the other farms, was advertised for sale. The slaves, livestock and equipment, household furnishings, books, and works of art were sold at auction. The last of the family abandoned Monticello in 1829. Two years passed before a buyer could be found. Already suffering from disrepair and neglect before Jefferson died, Monticello now fell to rack and ruin. Only the weather vane performed its accustomed work, said one traveler who was not alone in linking the fate of the house to Jefferson's supposed religious infidelity. "Monticello is rapidly fulfilling its destiny, as a naked, forsaken desolation." In 1831 James T. Barclay, a Charlottesville merchant, bought the house and 552 acres for approximately $7,000. Although Barclay had the money to improve the place and planned to cultivate silkworms on the mountain, he had no love for Jefferson or Monticello; and when large numbers of visitors continued to invade the property, peering in his windows, banging on his doors, Barclay decided to sell it.

The new owner, who took possession in 1836, was Lieutenant Uriah P. Levy of the United States Navy. He got a bargain: house, outbuildings, and 218 acres for $2,700. Levy revered Jefferson for his political principles, above all for the twin principles of religious freedom and separation of church and state. He commissioned the French sculptor David d'Angers to execute the first statue of Jefferson and offered it, unsuccessfully, to Congress in 1834. Levy added some two thousand acres to the estate, rehabilitated the mansion, and sought out original furnishings, paintings, and other memorabilia. For this reason he is remembered by his biographers as "The Savior of Monticello." The title is not without merit. Yet Levy, busily accumulating a fortune in the North and striving against great odds, as a Jew, to pursue his naval career, was never more than an occasional resident, and in the end, he made the mistake of placing the property in the beggarly custody of an overseer named Joel Wheeler. Wheeler scraped a living from the rundown lands, installed pigpens on the front lawn, and stored grain on the parquet floors of the parlor. He discouraged visitors by charging them a small fee. Still they came, pilgrims and scavengers, as many as ten thousand a year. The shameful defacement of Jefferson's tombstone was well known to the public. Now, it was said, the exterior walls of the house were covered with scribbled names. "Hundreds of them can be seen and read on each side of the front entrance to the hall; [inside] pieces of the bust of Mr. Jefferson were chipped off; chairs, tables, mirrors, vases, broken and destroyed."

Commodore Levy died in 1862, and the nadir of Monticello's fortunes began. He willed the property to the United States for use as a school for the orphan children of navy warrant officers. The Civil War was raging. Congress could not carry out the bequest even if it had accepted it. The Confederacy confiscated Monticello as alien property and in 1864 sold it at auction to Lieutenant Colonel Benjamin F. Ficklin, C.S.A., for 80,500 Confederate dollars. Although the property reverted to the United States the following year, Levy's heirs moved to break the will, as they had threatened to do from the beginning. The protracted litigation culminated in the decree of a Virginia court directing still another public sale of Monticello. The successful bidder was Jefferson M. Levy, the commodore's nephew, the only member of the family who cared for the place, and a prosperous New York lawyer. He paid $10,500 for the house and 218 acres. The day Levy took possession he dismissed Joel Wheeler, the careless steward of the property for twenty-one years.

Jefferson Levy has better claim than his uncle to the title of savior of Monticello. He lavished money and affection on the place and was generally in residence four to six months of every year. He regained several hundred acres of the original estate, hired an expert superintendent, Thomas L. Rhodes, and put house and grounds in good order again. He installed central heating and modern plumbing. He purchased Jefferson heirlooms—Sheraton card tables, a silver coffee urn, Wedgwood mantlepieces—that had been scattered through Albemarle County and beyond. These were returned to Monticello where they joined several precious pieces—the seven-day clock in the hall, the Louis XVI pier mirrors in the parlor—that, strangely enough, had never left the house. Finally, after some initial stumbling, Levy proved to be an accommodating host to a rising tide of visitors.

Still, good steward though he was, Monticello was Levy's home, not Jefferson's, not the nation's; and in time the whim and caprice of private ownership must prove intolerable. Upon entering, visitors were struck by the full-length portrait of Levy. The furnishings, the interior decor, were more in Levy's taste than Jefferson's. Outside, statues stood on the east lawn and sculptured lions guarded the west portico. Above the roofline balustrade piercing dormers could be observed, and at a later time ivy grew thick on the brick walls. As Monticello became more accessible by railroad and highway, as the fortunes of the Democratic party revived and leading Democrats celebrated the teachings of their putative father, as Monticello at last came to be appreciated as an architectural masterpiece, a movement arose to make it a national shrine under public ownership.

The first national leader to advance the claim of the American people to Jefferson's home was William Jennings Bryan. He made his pilgrimage to mecca as a young Nebraska congressman. (A decade earlier, in 1882, Congress had declared the nation's interest in Jefferson's grave by appropriating $10,000 to replace the granite monument that had been defaced and destroyed over the years.) When Levy rebuffed Bryan's overture, he backed off. In 1909 Maud Littleton, the wife of a New York congressman, mounted a crusade to make Monticello a national shrine. Three years later her Monticello Memorial Association, with widespread support, requested Congress to purchase the property. Levy, then himself a Democratic congressman from New York, remained adamant. "My answer to any proposition seeking the property of Monticello is: 'When the White House is for sale, then I will consider an offer for Monticello.'" Although Congress declined to act in 1912, the movement went forward, and within a few years Levy's defenses crumbled. He agreed to sell Monticello to the government for $500,000, which was half its estimated value. When Congress dragged its feet, he advertised Monticello for sale. Finally, in 1923, a newly chartered nonprofit corporation, the Thomas Jefferson Memorial Foundation, purchased the property—the house and some six hundred acres—for half a million dollars.

The number of visitors to Monticello, except for brief dips occasioned by war and depression, rose steadily from 50,000 in 1924 to 125,000 in 1941 and 200,000 in 1947. In the early years under the Foundation's stewardship, essential repairs of house and grounds took precedence over restoration work. In 1941 the mortgage was burned. As income rose after the Second World War, restoration began in earnest. The house underwent structural renovation, and the exterior again looked much as it had in Jefferson's day. With continued research and the return of many original furnishings and artifacts, the interior, too, resumed an appearance that would be familiar to Jefferson were he suddenly to materialize among the visitors. Thanks to the meticulous records he left, groves, orchards, and gardens have been restored until the entire landscape has become Jeffersonian. The present-day visitor responds to Monticello in the ways visitors have responded in the past; yet he or she responds with greater awareness of the man and his creation, for never before have they been so fully and so faithfully exposed to view.

"A Noble Spirit
of Building"

AMONG THE FIRST VISITORS to Monticello were the English and German officers of the Convention Army, surrendered at Saratoga and imprisoned at the Barracks outside Charlottesville, Virginia. Thomas Jefferson, who became governor of Virginia some months after they arrived, extended the hospitality of his home to them. The first announcement of Monticello's existence to the European world may have been in a letter of one of these German officers. Jacob Rubsamen, a German-speaking Virginian, forwarded a translation to Jefferson in December 1780.

IN A NEWSPAPER printed at Hamburg and enclosed in one of the Letters, I find the following extract of a German Officers Letter dated barracks—

My only Occupation at present, is, to learn the English Language, it is the easier for me as I have free Access to a Copious and well chosen Library of Colo. Jefferson's Governor of Virginia. The father of this learned Man's was also a favourite of the Muses. There is now a Map of his of Virginia extant, the best of the Kind. The Governor possesses a Noble Spirit of Building, he is now finishing an elegant building projected according to his own fancy. In his parlour he is creating on the Cieling a Compass of his own invention by wich he can Know the strenght as well as Direction of the Winds. I have promised to paint the Compass for it. He was much pleased with a fancy Painting of mine and particularly admired the Paper Money brought on in the piece, and in Joke often rebuked me for my thoughtlessness to shew him counterfeit money for wich I Knew many had been hanged allready. As all Virginians are fond of Music, he is particularly so. You will find in his House an Elegant harpsicord Piano forte and some Violins. The latter he performs well upon himself, the former his Lady touches very skilfully and who, is in all Respects a very agreable Sensible and Accomplished Lady.

Julian P. Boyd, ed., *The Papers of Thomas Jefferson* (Princeton, N.J., 1951—), 4:174. Copyright 1951, © 1979 renewed by Princeton University Press. Reprinted by permission.

⫷ 1782 ⫸

A Philosophical Encounter

IN APRIL 1782 the chevalier de Chastellux, a member of the French Academy, author of *De la Félicité Publique,* and an officer in General Rochambeau's army encamped at Williamsburg, arrived at Monticello on Jefferson's thirty-ninth birthday and stayed for several days. Chastellux saw the original house in nearly completed form. His charming portrait of its master was the first to present Jefferson to the world in philosophical colors. It appeared in Chastellux's travel journal published in Paris in 1786 and the next year in an English translation, *Travels in North America.* The following version is taken from Howard Rice's edition and translation of 1963.

April 13, 1782: Boswell's Tavern—Monticello
I SET OUT THE NEXT MORNING at eight o'clock, having learned nothing in this house worthy of remark, except that notwithstanding the hale and robust appearance of Mr. and Mrs. Boswell, not one of their fourteen children had attained the age of two. We were now approaching a chain of mountains of considerable height, called the South-west Mountains, because they are the first you meet in traveling westward before reaching the chain known in France as the Appalachians and in Virginia as the Blue Ridge, North Ridge [North Mountain], and Alleghany Mountains. As the country is heavily wooded we seldom had a view of them. I traveled a long time without seeing any habitation and was at a loss to know which of the many crossroads to take. At last I overtook a traveler who had preceded us and he not only served as my guide, but also made the journey seem less long by his

company. He was an Irishman, who though but lately arrived in America, had served in several campaigns and had received a considerable wound in his thigh. He told me that they had never been able to extract the bullet, but he was none the less in good health and spirits. I got him to tell me about his military exploits, and particularly asked for details about the country where he now lives, for he had told me that he was settled in North Carolina, upwards of eighty miles from Catawba and more than 300 from the seacoast. . . . It was a natural question to ask this farmer what could take him four hundred miles from home, and I learned that he was carrying on the only trade possible in his country and by which the people who are the best off seek to increase their income—that of selling horses. Indeed, these animals multiply very fast in regions where there is abundant pasturage; and as they can be driven with no expense, by letting them graze along the way, they are the most convenient article of exportation for localities distant from the main roads and from the trading centers.

The conversation continued between us and brought us imperceptibly to the foot of the mountains. We had no difficulty in recognizing on one of the summits the house of Mr. Jefferson, for it may be said that "it shines alone in this secluded spot." He himself built it and chose the site, for although he already owned fairly extensive lands in the neighborhood, there was nothing, in such an unsettled country, to prevent him from fixing his residence wherever he wanted to. But Nature so contrived it, that a Sage and a man of taste should find on his own estate the spot where he might best study and enjoy Her. He called this house *Monticello* (in Italian, Little Mountain), a very modest name indeed, for it is situated upon a very high mountain, but a name which bespeaks the owner's attachment to the language of Italy and above all to the Fine Arts, of which Italy was the cradle and is still the resort.

As I had no further occasion for a guide, I parted ways with my Irishman, and after continuing uphill for more than half an hour by a rather good road, I arrived at Monticello. This house, of which Mr. Jefferson was the architect, and often the builder, is constructed in an Italian style, and is quite tasteful, although not however without some faults; it consists of a large square pavilion, into which one enters through two porticoes ornamented with columns.[1] The ground floor consists chiefly of a large and lofty *salon*, or drawing room, which is to be decorated entirely in the antique style; above the *salon* is a library of the same form; two small wings, with only a ground floor and attic, are joined to this pavilion, and are intended to communicate with the kitchen, offices, etc, which will form on either side a kind of basement topped by a terrace. My object in giving these details is not to describe the house, but to prove that it resembles none of the others seen in this country; so that it may be said that Mr. Jefferson is the first American who has consulted the Fine Arts to know how he should shelter himself from the weather. But it is with him alone that I should concern myself.

Let me then describe to you a man, not yet forty, tall, and with a mild and pleasing countenance, but whose mind and attainments could serve in lieu of all outward graces; an American, who, without ever having quitted his own country, is Musician, Draftsman, Surveyor, Astronomer, Natural Philosopher, Jurist, and Statesman; a Senator of America, who sat for two years in that famous Congress which brought about the Revolution and which is never spoken of here without respect—though with a respect unfortunately mingled with too many misgivings; a Governor of Virginia, who filled this difficult station during the invasions of Arnold, Phillips, and Cornwallis; and finally a Philosopher, retired from the world and public business, because he loves the world only insofar as he can feel that he is useful, and because the temper of his fellow citizens is not as yet prepared either to face the truth or to suffer contradiction. A gentle and amiable wife, charming children whose education is his special care, a house to embellish, extensive estates to improve, the arts and sciences to cultivate—these are what remain to Mr. Jefferson, after having played a distinguished role on the stage of the New World, and what he has preferred to the honorable commission of Minister Plenipotentiary in Europe.

April 14–16, 1782: At Monticello

The visit which I made Mr. Jefferson was not unexpected, for he had long since invited me to come and spend a few days in his company, that is, amid the mountains. Nevertheless I at first found his manner grave and even cold; but I had no sooner spent two hours with him than I felt as if we had spent our whole lives together. Walking, the library—and above all, conversation which was always varied, always interesting, always sustained by that sweet satisfaction experienced by two persons who in communicating their feelings and opinions invariably find themselves in agreement and who understand each other at the first hint—all these made my four days spent at Monticello seem like four minutes.

This conformity of feelings and opinions, on which I dwell because it was a source of satisfaction to me and because egotism must now and then appear, this conformity, I repeat, was so perfect that not only our tastes were similar, but our predilections also—those predilections or partialities which cold and methodical minds hold up to ridicule as mere "enthusiasm," but which men of spirit and feeling take pride in calling by this very name of "enthusiasm." I recall with pleasure that as we were conversing one evening over a "bowl of punch," after Mrs. Jefferson had retired, we happened to speak of the poetry of Ossian. It was a spark of electricity which passed rapidly from one to the other; we recalled the passages of those sublime poems which had particularly struck us, and we recited them for the benefit of my traveling companions, who fortunately knew English well and could appreciate them, even though they had never read the poems. Soon the book was called for, to share in our "toasts": it was brought forth and placed beside the bowl of punch. And, before we realized it, book and bowl carried us far into the night. At other times, natural philosophy was the subject of our conversations, and at still others, politics or the arts, for no object has escaped Mr. Jefferson; and it seems indeed as though, ever since his youth, he had placed his mind, like his house, on a lofty height, whence he might contemplate the whole universe.

The only stranger who visited us during our stay at Monticello was Colonel Armand whom I have mentioned in my first journal.[2] As my friends know, he went to France last year [1781] with Colonel [John] Laurens, but returned in time to be present at the siege of Yorktown, where he marched as a volunteer in the attack on the redoubts. His object in going to France was to purchase clothing and complete equipment for a legion that he had already commanded, but which had been broken up in the southern campaigns, so that it was necessary to form anew. He himself advanced the necessary funds to Congress, which agreed to provide the men and the horses. Charlottesville, a rising little town situated in a valley two leagues from Monticello, is the headquarters assigned for assembling this legion. Colonel Armand invited me to dine with him the next day; I went there with Mr. Jefferson, and found the legion under arms. It is to be composed of 200 horses and 150 foot. The cavalry was almost complete and fairly well mounted; the infantry was still much below full strength, but the whole was well clothed, well armed, and made a very good appearance. We dined at Colonel Armand's with all the officers of his regiment, and with his wolf, for he has made a pastime of raising a wolf, which is now ten months old, and is as familiar, mild, and gay as a young dog. The wolf never leaves his master, and even has the privilege of sharing his bed. I hope that he will still reflect his good upbringing and not revert to his natural character when he has come to wolf's estate. He is not quite of the same kind as ours, for his coat is almost black and very smooth; so that there is nothing fierce about his head, and were it not for his upright ears and pendant tail, one might easily take him for a dog. Perhaps he owes the singular advantage of not exhaling a bad smell to the care which is taken of his toilet, for I noticed that the dogs were not in the least afraid of him and that when they crossed his track they paid no attention to it. Now it is difficult for me to believe that all the cleanliness possible can deceive the instinct of these animals, which have such a dread of wolves, that they have been observed at the *Jardin du Roi* in Paris to bristle up and howl at the mere smell of two mongrels born of a dog and a she-wolf. I am inclined therefore to believe that this peculiarity belongs only to the species of black wolf, for you also see in America species similar to ours. It may be that we also have in Europe something like the American black kind; one might at least so conclude from the common saying, "*il a peur de moi comme du loup gris* (he is as much afraid of me as of a grey wolf)," which would imply that there were also black wolves.

Since I am on the subject of animals, I shall mention here some observations which Mr. Jefferson enabled me to make upon the only wild animals which are common in this country. I was long in doubt whether they should be called *chevreuils* (roe deer), *cerfs* (hart), or *daims* (deer), for in Canada they are known by the first name, in the eastern provinces by the second, and in the south by the third. Besides, in America, nomenclatures are so inexact, and observations so rare, that no information can be acquired by querying the people of the country. Mr. Jefferson having amused himself by raising a score of these animals in a park, they soon became very tame, which happens to all American animals, which are in general much more easily tamed than those of Europe. He enjoys feeding them with Indian corn, of which they are very fond, and which they eat out of his hand. I followed him one evening into a deep valley where they are accustomed to assemble towards the close of the day. I watched them walk, run, and bound; and the more I examined their paces, the less I was inclined to annex them to any European species: they are of absolutely the same color as the *chevreuil,* and this color never varies from one individual to another, even when they are tamed, as often happens with our *daims.* Their horns, which are never more than a foot and a half long, and never have more than three or four branches on each side, are more open and broader than those of the *chevreuil.* They differ also from the *chevreuil* in that they never go in pairs, but gather in herds as do our *cerfs* and *daims.* From my own observations, in short, and from all I have been able to collect on the subject, I am convinced that this species is peculiar to America, and that it may be considered as somewhere in between the *daim* and the *chevreuil.*

Mr. Jefferson being no sportsman, and never having crossed the seas, could have no definite opinion on this point of natural history; but he has not neglected the other branches. I saw with pleasure that he had applied himself in particular to meteorological observation, which, in fact, of all the branches of natural philosophy, is the most appropiate for Americans to cultivate, because the extent of their country and the variety of sites give them in this particular a great advantage over us, who in other respects have so many over them. Mr. Jefferson has made, with Mr. Madison [president of the College of William and Mary], a well-informed professor of mathematics, some corresponding observations on the prevailing winds at Williamsburg and at Monticello; and although these two places are only fifty leagues distant from each other and are not separated by any chain of mountains, the difference between the results was that for 127 observations of the northeast wind at Williamsburg there were only 32 at Monticello, where the northwest wind in general took the place of the northeast. This latter appears to be a seawind, easily counteracted by the slightest obstacle, insomuch that twenty years ago it was scarcely ever felt beyond West Point, that is, beyond the confluence of the Pamunkey and the Mattaponi which unite to form the York River about thirty-five miles from its mouth. Since the progress of population and agriculture has considerably cleared the woods, this northeast wind penetrates as far as Richmond, which is thirty miles further inland. It may thus be observed, first, that the winds vary greatly in their obliquity and in the height of their regions; and, secondly, that nothing is more important than the manner in which the clearing of a country is undertaken, for the salubrity of the air, even the order of the seasons, may depend on the access allowed to the winds and the direction given to them. It is a generally accepted opinion in Rome that the air there is less healthy since the cutting of a large forest which used to be situated between that city and Ostia and which protected it from the winds known in Italy as the *Scirocco* and the *Libico*. It is also believed in Spain that the excessive droughts, of which the Castilians complain more and more, are occasioned by the cutting down of the woods, which used to stop and break up the clouds. There is still another very important consideration upon which I thought fit to call to the attention of the learned in this country, whatever diffidence I may have of my own knowledge in natural philosophy, as in every other subject. The greatest part of Virginia is very low and flat, and so divided by creeks and great rivers, that it appears in fact redeemed from the sea and entirely of very recent creation; it is therefore swampy, and can be dried only by cutting down many woods; but as on the other hand it can never be so drained as not still to abound in mephitic exhalations; and of whatever nature these exhalations may be, whether partaking of fixed or inflammable air, it is certain that vegetation absorbs them equally, and that trees are the most proper to accomplish this object.[3] It therefore appears equally dangerous either to cut down or to preserve a great quantity of wood; so that the best manner of proceeding to clear the country would be to disperse the settlements as much as possible, and always to leave some groves of trees standing between them. In this manner the ground inhabited would always be made healthy; and as there will still remain considerable marshes which cannot be drained, there will be no risk of admitting too easily the winds which blow the exhalations from them.

April 17, 1782: Departure from Monticello

But I perceive that my journal is something like the conversation I had with Mr. Jefferson. I pass from one object to another, and forget myself as I write, as it happened not unfrequently in his society. I must now take leave of the Friend of Nature, but not of Nature herself, for she expects me in all her splendor at the goal of my journey—I refer to that famous "rock bridge"[4] which joins two mountains, the greatest curiosity that I have ever beheld, because it is one of the most difficult to account for. Mr. Jefferson would most willingly have taken me there, although this wonder with which he is perfectly acquainted is more than eighty miles from his home; but his wife was expecting her confinement at any moment, and he is as good a husband as he is a philosopher and citizen. He therefore only acted as my guide for about sixteen miles, as far as the crossing of the little Mechum River. Here we parted, and I presume to believe that it was with mutual regret.

Marquis de Chastellux, *Travels in North America in the Years 1780, 1781, and 1782*, tr. and ed. Howard C. Rice, Jr. (Chapel Hill, N.C., 1963), 2:389–96. © 1963 The University of North Carolina Press. Published for the Institute of Early American History and Culture, Williamsburg. Reprinted by permission.

1. This is evidence that at least one of the two-story porticoes was in place.

2. *Journey from Newport, to Philadelphia, Albany, &c.*, published in 1781.

3. The theory of American climate here set forth resembles that of the comte de Buffon, which Jefferson refuted in *Notes on Virginia* (1785).

4. Natural Bridge, in Rockbridge County.

⁊

A Touring Irishman
on the Mountain

JEFFERSON evidently was absent when Isaac Weld, Jr., traveling the road from Richmond, stopped at Monticello in May
1796. Earlier in the year Jefferson had commenced his "dem-
olitions," and the house was in disarray. Weld, a young Irishman, was attentive to such mundane matters as soil and
climate, productions, and living conditions. His *Travels
through the States of North America,* published in London in
1799, was full of information useful to prospective immi-
grants. In the light of today's booming wine industry in Albemarle and surrounding counties, Weld's account of earlier
failures, Jefferson's among them, is interesting.

THE SOUTH-WEST MOUNTAINS run nearly parallel to the Blue Ridge,
and are the first which you come to on going up the country from the
sea-coast in Virginia. These mountains are not lofty, and ought indeed
rather be called hills than mountains; they are not seen till you come
within a very few miles of them, and the ascent is so gradual, that you
get upon their top almost without perceiving it. . . .
 Among these mountains live several gentlemen of large landed
property, who farm their own estates, as in the lower parts of Virginia;
among the number is Mr. Jefferson from whose seat I date this letter.
His house is about three miles distant from Charlottesville and two
from Milton, which is on the head waters of Rivanna River. It is most
singularly situated, being built upon the top of a small mountain, the
apex of which has been cut off, so as to leave an area of about an acre
and half. At present it is in an unfinished state; but if carried on ac-

cording to the plan laid down, it will be one of the most elegant private habitations in the United States. A large apartment is laid out for a library and museum, meant to extend the entire breadth of the house, the windows of which are to open into an extensive green house and aviary. In the center is another very spacious apartment, of an octagon form, reaching from the front to the rear of the house, the large folding glass doors of which, at each end, open under a portico. An apartment like this, extending from front to back, is very common in a Virginia house; it is called a saloon, and during summer is the one generally preferred by the family, on account of its being more airy and spacious than any other. The house commands a magnificent prospect on either side of the blue ridge of mountains for nearly forty miles, and on the opposite one, of the low country, in appearance like an extended heath covered with trees, the tops alone of which are visible. The mists and vapours arising from the low grounds give a continual variety to the scene. The mountain whereon the house stands is thickly wooded on one side, and walks are carried round it, with different degrees of obliquity, running into each other. On the south side is the garden and a large vineyard, that produces an abundance of fine fruit.

Several attempts have been made in this neighbourhood to bring the manufacture of wine to perfection; none of them however have succeeded to the wish of the parties. A set of gentlemen once went to the expence even of getting six Italians over for the purpose, but the vines which the Italians found growing here were different, as well as the soil, from what they had been in the habit of cultivating, and they were not much more successful in the business than the people of the country.[1] We must not, however, from hence conclude that good wine can never be manufactured upon these mountains. It is well known that the vines, and the mode of cultivating them, vary as much in different parts of Europe as the soil in one country differs from that in another. It will require some time, therefore, and different experiments, to ascertain the particular kind of vine, and the mode of cultivating it, best adapted to the soil and these mountains. This, however, having been once ascertained, there is every reason to suppose that the grape may be cultivated to the greatest perfection, as the climate is as favourable for the purpose as that of any country in Europe. By experiments also it is by no means improbable, that they will in process of time learn the best method of converting the juice of the fruit into wine.

Isaac Weld, Jr., *Travels through the States of North America during the Years 1795, 1796, and 1797* (London, 1799), 1:203, 206–9.

1. The reference is apparently to Philip Mazzei who came to Virginia in 1773 and, with ten vignerons from his native Tuscany, commenced experiments in viniculture in Jefferson's neighborhood.

⌐◁ 1 7 9 6 ▷⌐

A Frenchman Views
Jefferson the Farmer

CLOSE ON WELD'S heels came the duc de La Rochefoucauld-
Liancourt. Jefferson had become acquainted with this noble-
man of distinguished lineage in Paris. In 1789 he had been a
leader of the French Revolution. Now he was in exile. The
duke traveled extensively in the United States. His account of
a week's visit at Monticello during the harvest season of 1796
is especially valuable for its observations of Jefferson the
farmer. Although he formed a low opinion of Virginia agriculture generally and was skeptical of some of Jefferson's
ideas, he saw in him an American counterpart of Europe's
"improving landlord." La Rochefoucauld-Liancourt's *Travels
though the United States of America* appeared in an English
translation in 1799.

MONTICELLO is situated four miles from Milford, in that chain of
mountains which stretches from James's-River to the Rappahannock,
twenty-eight miles in front of the Blue-Ridge, and in a direction parallel to those mountains. This chain, which runs uninterrupted in its
small extent, assumes successively the names of West, South, and
Green Mountains.

It is the part known by the name of the South-Mountains that Monticello is situated. The house stands on the summit of the mountain,
and the taste and arts of Europe have been consulted in the formation
of its plan. Mr. Jefferson had commenced its construction before the
American revolution; since that epocha his life has been constantly
engaged in public affairs, and he has not been able to complete the

execution to the whole extent of the project which it seems he had at first conceived. That part of the building which was finished has suffered from the suspension of the work, and Mr. Jefferson, who two years since resumed the habits and leisure of private life, is now employed in repairing the damage occasioned by this interruption, and still more by his absence; he continues his original plan, and even improves on it, by giving to his buildings more elevation and extent. He intends that they should consist of only one story, crowned with balustrades; and a dome is to be constructed in the centre of the structure. The apartments will be large and convenient; the decoration, both outside and inside, simple, yet regular and elegant. Monticello, according to its first plan, was infinitely superior to all other houses in America, in point of taste and convenience; but at that time Mr. Jefferson had studied taste and the fine arts in books only. His travels in Europe have supplied him with models; he has appropriated them to his design; and his new plan, the execution of which is already much advanced, will be accomplished before the end of next year, and then the house will certainly deserve to be ranked with the most pleasant mansions in France and England.

Mr. Jefferson's house commands one of most extensive prospects you can meet with. On the east side, the front of the building, the eye is not checked by any object, since the mountain on which the house is seated, commands all the neighbouring heights as far as the Chesapeake. The Atlantic might be seen were it not for the greatness of the distance, which renders that prospect impossible. On the right and left the eye commands the extensive valley that separates the Green, South and West Mountains from the Blue-Ridge, and has no other bounds but these high mountains, of which, on a clear day you discern the chain on the right upwards of a hundred miles, far beyond James's-River; and on the left as far as Maryland, on the other side of the Potowmack. Through some intervals, formed by the irregular summits of the Blue-Mountains, you discover the Peaked-Ridge, a chain of mountains placed between the Blue and North Mountains, another more distant ridge. But in the back part the prospect is soon interrupted by a mountain more elevated than that on which the house is seated. The bounds of the view on this point, at so small a distance, form a pleasant resting-place; as the immensity of prospect it enjoys is, perhaps, already too vast. A considerable number of cultivated fields, houses, and barns, enliven and variegate the extensive land-scape, still more embellished by the beautiful and diversified forms of mountains, in the whole chain of which not one resembles another. The aid of fancy is, however, required to complete the enjoyment of this magnificent view; and she must picture to us those plains and mountains such as population and culture will render them in a greater or smaller number of years. The disproportion existing be-tween the cultivated lands and those which are still covered with for-ests as ancient as the globe, is at present much too great: and even when that shall have been done away, the eye may perhaps further wish to discover a broad river, a great mass of water—destitute of which, the grandest and most extensive prospect is ever destitute of an embellishment requisite to render it completely beautiful.

On this mountain, and in the surrounding valleys, on both banks of the Rivanna, are situated the five thousand acres of land which Mr. Jefferson possesses in this part of Virginia. Eleven hundred and twenty only are cultivated. The land left to the care of stewards has suffered as well as the buildings from the long absence of the master; according to the custom of the country it has been exhausted by successive cul-ture. Its situation on declivities of hills and mountains renders a care-ful cultivation more necessary than is requisite in lands situated in a flat and even country; the common routine is more pernicious, and more judgment and mature thought are required, than in a different soil. This forms at present the chief employment of Mr. Jefferson. But little accustomed to agricultural pursuits, he has drawn the principles of culture either from works which treat on this subject, or from con-versation. Knowledge thus acquired often misleads, and is at all times insufficient in a country where agriculture is well understood; yet it is preferable to mere practical knowledge, in a country where a bad practice prevails, and where it is dangerous to follow the routine, from which it is so difficult to depart. Above all, much good may be ex-pected, if a contemplative mind, like that of Mr. Jefferson, which takes the theory for its guide, watches its application with discernment, and rectifies it according to the peculiar circumstances and nature of the country, climate and soil, and conformably to the experience which he daily acquires.

Pursuant to the ancient rotation tobacco was cultivated four or five successive years; the land was then suffered to lie fallow, and then again succeeded crops of tobacco. The culture of tobacco being now almost entirely relinquished in this part of Virginia, the common rotation begins with wheat, followed by Indian corn, and then again wheat, until the exhausted soil loses every productive power; the field is then abandoned, and the cultivator proceeds to another, which he treats and abandons in the same manner, until he returns to the first, which has in the mean time recovered some of its productive faculties. The disproportion between the quantity of land which belongs to the planters and the hands they can employ in its culture, diminishes the inconveniences of this detestable method. The land, which never receives the least manure, supports a longer or shorter time this alternate cultivation of wheat and Indian corn, according to its nature and situation, and regains, according to the same circumstances, more or less speedily the power of producing new crops. If in the interval it be covered with heath and weeds, it frequently is again fit for cultivation at the end of eight or ten years; if not, a space of twenty years is not sufficient to render it capable of production. Planters who are not possessed of a sufficient quantity of land to let so much of it remain unproductive for such a length of time, fallow it in a year or two after it has borne wheat and Indian corn, during which time the fields serve as pasture, and are hereupon again cultivated in the same manner. In either case the land produces from five to six bushels of wheat, or from ten to fifteen bushels of Indian corn, the acre. To the produce of Indian corn must also be added one hundred pounds of leaves to every five bushels, or each barrel, of grain. These leaves are given as fodder to the cattle. It was in this manner that Mr. Jefferson's land had always been cultivated, and it is this system which he has very wisely relinquished. He has divided all his land under culture into four farms, and every farm into six fields of forty acres. Each farm consists, therefore, of two hundred and eighty acres. His system of rotation embraces seven years, and this is the reason why each farm has been divided into seven fields. In the first of these seven years wheat is cultivated; in the second, Indian corn; in the third, pease or potatoes; in the fourth, vetches; in the fifth, wheat; in the sixth and seventh, clover. Thus each of his fields yields some produce every year, and his rotation of successive culture, while it prepares the soil for the following crop, increases its produce. The abundance of clover, potatoes, pease, &c. will enable him to keep sufficient cattle for manuring his land, which at present receives hardly any dung at all, independently of the great profit which he will in the future derive from the sale of his cattle.

Each farm, under the direction of a particular steward or bailiff, is cultivated by four negroes, four negresses, four oxen, and four horses. The bailiffs, who in general manage their farms separately, assist each other during the harvest, as well as at any other time, when there is any pressing labour. The great declivity of the fields, which would render it extremely troublesome and tedious to carry the produce, even of each farm, to one central point, has induced Mr. Jefferson to construct on each field a barn, sufficiently capacious to hold its produce in grain; the produce in forage is also housed there, but this is generally so great, that it becomes necessary to make stacks near the barns. The latter are constructed of trunks of trees, and the floors are boarded. The forests and slaves reduce the expence of these buildings to a mere trifle.

Mr. Jefferson possesses one of those excellent threshing-machines, which a few years since were invented in Scotland, and are already very common in England. This machine, the whole of which does not weigh two thousand pounds, is conveyed from one barn to another in a waggon, and threshes from one hundred and twenty to one hundred and fifty bushels a day. A worm, whose eggs are almost constantly deposited in the ear of the grain, renders it necessary to thresh the corn a short time after the harvest; in this case the heat, occasioned by the mixture of grain with its envelope, from which it is disengaged, but with which it continues mixed, destroys the vital principle of the egg, and protects the corn from the inconveniences of its being hatched. If the grain continued in the ears, without being speedily beaten, it would be destroyed by the worm, which would be excluded from the eggs. This scourge, however, spreads no farther northwards than the Potowmack, and is bounded to the west by the Blue Mountains.[1] A few weeks after the corn has been beaten, it is free from all danger, winnowed and sent to market. The Virginia planters have generally their corn trodden out by horses; but this way is slow, and there is no country in the world where this operation requires more dispatch than in this part of Virginia. Besides the straw is bruised by the treading of horses. Mr. Jefferson hopes that his machine, which has already found some imitators among his neighbours, will be generally adopted in Virginia. In a country where all the inhabitants possess plenty of wood, this machine may be made at a very trifling expence.

Mr. Jefferson rates the average produce of an acre of land, in the present state of his farm, at eight bushels of wheat, eighteen bushels of Indian corn, and twenty hundred weight of clover. After the land has been duly manured, he may expect a produce twice, nay three times more considerable. But his land will never be dunged as much as in Europe. Black cattle and pigs, which in our country are either constantly kept on the farm, or at least return thither every evening, and whose dung is carefully gathered and preserved either separate or mixed, according to circumstances, are here left grazing in the woods the whole year round. Mr Jefferson keeps no more sheep than are necessary for the consumption of his own table. He cuts his clover but twice each season, and does not suffer his cattle to graze in his fields. The quantity of his dung is therefore in proportion to the number of cattle which he can keep with his own fodder, and which he intends to buy at the beginning of winter to sell them again in spring; and the cattle kept in the vicinity of the barns where the forage is housed, will furnish manure only for the adjacent fields.

From an opinion entertained by Mr. Jefferson, that the heat of the sun destroys, or at least dries up in a great measure, the nutritious juices of the earth, he judges it necessary that it should be always covered. In order therefore to preserve his fields, as well as to multiply their produce, they never lie fallow. On the same principle he cuts his clover but twice a season, does not let the cattle feed on the grass, nor incloses his fields, which are merely divided by a single row of peach trees.

A long experience would be required to form a correct judgment, whether the loss of dung which this system occasions in his farms, and the known advantage of fields enclosed with ditches, especially in a declivous situation, where the earth from the higher grounds is constantly washed down by the rain, are fully compensated by the vegetative powers which he means thus to preserve in his fields. His system is entirely confined to himself; it is censured by some of his neighbours, who are also employed in improving their culture with ability and skill, but he adheres to it, and thinks it is founded on just observations.

Wheat, as has already been observed, is the chief object of cultivation in this country. The rise, which within these two years has taken place in the price of this article, has engaged the speculations of the planters, as well as the merchants. The population of Virginia, which is so inconsiderable in proportion to its extent, and so little collected in towns, would offer but a very precarious market for large numbers of cattle. Every planter has as many of them in the woods as are required for the consumption of his family. The negroes, who form a considerable part of the population, eat but little meat, and this little is pork. Some farmers cultivate rye and oats, but they are few in number. Corn is sold here to the merchants of Milford or Charlotte-Ville, who ship it for Richmond, where it fetches a shilling more per bushel than in other places. Speculation or a pressing want of money may at times occasion variations in this manner of sale, but it is certainly the most common way. Money is very scarce in this district, and, bank-notes being unknown, trade is chiefly carried on by barter; the merchant, who receives the grain, returns its value in such commodities the vender stands in need of.

Mr. Jefferson sold his wheat last year for two dollars and a half per bushel. He contends, that it is in this district whiter than in the environs of Richmond, and all other low countries, and that one bushel, which weighs there only fifty-five to fifty-eight pounds, weighs on his farm from sixty to sixty-five.

In addition to the eleven hundred and twenty acres of land, divided into four farms, Mr. Jefferson sows a few acres with turnips, succory, and other seeds.

Before I leave his farm, I shall not forget to mention, that I have seen here a *drilling machine*, the name of which cannot be translated into French but by *machine à femer en paguets."* By Mr. Jefferson's account, it has been invented in his neighbourhood. If this machine fully answers the good opinion which he entertains of it, the invention is the more fortunate, as by Arthur Young's assertion not one good drilling-machine is to be found in England. This machine, placed on a sort of plough-carriage, carries an iron, which gently opens the furrow as deeply as it required. Behind this iron, and in the upper part of the machine, is a small trough, containing the grain which is intended to be sown. This grain is taken out of the trough by a row of small receivers, sewed on a leather band, or ribbon, and turning round two pivots placed above each other at the distance of from seven to eight inches. The small receivers take the grain from the trough, and turn it over into a small conduit, which conveys it into the furrow made by the iron. The distance of one of those receivers from another determines that of the places in which the grain is deposited in the ground; and a harrow, fixed on the machine behind the conduits through which the feed falls into the furrow, covers it again. The *endless* chain of the receivers, which forms the merit of the machine, may be compared with that which is used for drawing water from a great depth, or still more properly with a heaver of flour in Evans's mills.[2] It is put in motion by a light wheel, which moves along the ground as the machine advances, and is fixed in such a manner that it is not obstructed in its movements by the inequalities of the ground, nor even by the stones which it may find in its way. If this machine really answers the intended purpose, it is difficult to conceive why it should not have been invented before, as it is extremely simple, composed of movements well known, and of powers frequently employed. In my opinion it admits, however, of great improvements. . . .

In private life Mr. Jefferson displays a mild, easy and obliging temper, though he is somewhat cold and reserved. His conversation is of the most agreeable kind, and he possesses a stock of information not inferior to that of any other man. In Europe he would hold a distinguished rank among men of letters, and as such he has already appeared there; at present he is employed with activity and perseverance in the management of his farms and buildings; and he orders, directs, and pursues in the minutest detail every branch of business relative to them. I found him in the midst of the harvest, from which the scorching heat of the sun does not prevent his attendance. His negroes are nourished, clothed, and treated as well as white servants could be. As he cannot expect any assistance from the two small neighbouring towns, every article is made on his farm; his negroes are cabinetmakers, carpenters, masons, bricklayers, smiths, &c. The children he employs in a nail-manufactory, which yields already a considerable profit. The young and old negresses spin for the clothing of the rest. He animates them by rewards and distinctions; in fine, his superior mind directs the management of his domestic concerns with the same abilities, activity, and regularity, which he evinced in the conduct of public affairs, and which he is calculated to display in every situation of life. In the superintendence of his household he is assisted by his two daughters, Mrs. *Randolph* and Miss *Mary*, who are handsome, modest, and amiable women. They have been educated in France. Their father went often with them to the house of Madame *d'Enville*, my dear and respectable aunt, where they became acquainted with my family, and as the names of many of my friends are not unknown to them, we were able to converse of them together. It will be easily conceived, that this could not but excite in my mind strong sensations, and recollections, sometimes painful, yet generally sweet. Fifteen hundred leagues from our native country, in another world, and frequently given up to melancholy, we fancy ourselves restored to existence, and not utter strangers to happiness, when we hear our family and our friends mentioned by persons who have known them, who repeat their names, describe their persons, and express themselves on so interesting a subject in terms of kindness and benevolence.

Mr. Randolph is proprietor of a considerable plantation, contiguous to that of Mr. Jefferson's; he constantly spends the summer with him, and, from the affection he bears him, he seems to be his son rather than his son-in-law. Miss Maria constantly resides with her father; but as she is seventeen years old, and is remarkably handsome, she will, doubtless, soon find, that there are duties which it is still sweeter to perform than those of a daughter. Mr. Jefferson's philosophic turn of mind, his love of study, his excellent library, which supplies him with the means of satisfying it, and his friends, will undoubtedly help him to endure this loss, which moreover is not likely to become an absolute privation, as the second son-in-law of Mr. Jefferson may, like Mr. Randolph, reside in the vicinity of Monticello, and, if he be worthy of Miss Maria, will not be able to find any company more desirable than that of Mr. Jefferson.

The situation of Monticello exempts this place from the pestilential effluvia which produce so many diseases in the lower countries. From its great elevation it enjoys the purest air; and the sea-breeze, which is felt on shore about eight or nine o'clock in the morning, reaches Monticello at one or two in the afternoon, and somewhat refreshes the atmosphere, but the sun is intolerable from its scorching heat; as indeed it is in all the southern States. The places that enjoy some advantage over others are those which, like Monticello, are exposed to its direct rays, without experiencing their reflection from more elevated mountains, or neighbouring buildings.

Mr. Jefferson, in common with all landholders in America, imagines that his habitation is more healthy than any other; that it is as healthful as any in the finest parts of France; and that neither the ague, nor any other bilious distempers are ever observed at Monticello. This is undoubtedly true, because he asserts it, in regard to himself, to his family, and his negroes, none of whom is attacked by these maladies; but I am, nevertheless, of opinion, that a European, who during this season should expose himself too much to the air from nine in the morning until six at night, would not long enjoy a good state of health. During the seven days I continued there, not one passed without some moments of rain, and yet the intensity of the heat was not in the least abated by it.

In Virginia mongrel negroes are found in greater number than in Carolina and Georgia; and I have even seen, especially at Mr. Jefferson's, slaves, who, neither in point of colour nor features, shewed the least trace of their original descent; but their mothers being slaves, they retain, of consequence, the same condition. This superior number of people of colour is owing to the superior antiquity of the settlement of Virginia, and to the class of stewards or bailiffs, who are accused of producing this mongrel breed. They are liable to temptation, because they are young, and constantly amidst their slaves; and they enjoy the power of gratifying their passions, because they are despots. But the public opinion is so much against this intercourse between the white people and the black, that it is always by stealth, and transiently, the former satisfy their desires, as no white man is known to live regularly with a black woman.

Before I close this article I must say, that during my residence at Monticello I witnessed the indignation excited in all the planters of the neighborhood by the cruel conduct of a master to his slave, whom he had flogged to such a degree as to leave him almost dead on the spot. Justice pursues this barbarous master, and all the other planters declared loudly their wish, that he may be severely punished, which seems not to admit of any doubt.

But it is time to take leave of Mr. Jefferson, whose kind reception has perfectly answered what I had a right to expect from his civility, from our former acquaintance in France, and from his particular connection with my relations and friends. Mr. Jefferson is invited by the republican party, named anti-federalists, to succeed George Washington in the President's chair of the United States, the latter having publicly declared, that he will not continue in this place, although he should be re-elected by the majority of the people of the United States. The other party is desirous of raising John Adams to that station, whose past services, and distinguished conduct in the cause of liberty, together with his place of Vice-President, give him also, no doubt, very powerful claims. In the present situation of the United States, divided as they are between two parties, which mutually accuse each other of perfidy and treason, and involved in political measures which it is equally difficult to retract and to pursue, this exalted station is surrounded with dangerous rocks; probity, a zealous attachment to the public cause, and the most eminent abilities, will not be sufficient to steer clear of them all. There exists no more in the United States a man in a situation similar to that of George Washington. On his first election, the confidence and gratitude of all America were concentrated in him. Such a man cannot exist in the present conjuncture of circumstances, and the next president of the United States will be only the president of a party. Without being the enemy of one of the pretenders, one cannot, therefore, concur in the wish which he may entertain of being elevated to that eminent post. The fleeting enjoyment of the vanity of him, who shall be elected president, may, perhaps, be followed by the keenest pangs of grief in his remaining days.

The two small towns of Charlotte-Ville and Milford trade in the produce of the country situated between them and the mountains. They also form a sort of depôt for the commodities of more distant parts of the country; especially Milford, where the navigation begins, and does not experience any farther interruption from this point to Richmond. The water-carriage of merchandize and commodities costs one third of a dollar per hundred weight. The trade, which in a small degree is also carried on with money, is chiefly managed by barter, because money is scarce, and notes are not readily received. The price of land is from four to five dollars per acre, and the quantity of land to be sold is very considerable. Meat, that is, mutton, veal and lamb, fetches fourpence a pound; beef cannot be had but in winter. The wages of white workmen, such as masons, carpenters, cabinetmakers, and smiths, amount to from one and a half dollar to two dollars a day, according as they are scarce in the country. During the present season masons obtain the highest pay; there are not four stonemasons in the whole county of Albemarle, where Monticello is situated, which I left on the 29th of June.

Duc de La Rochefoucauld-Liancourt, *Travels through the United States of North America* (London, 1799), 2:69–77, 79–84.

1. The grain was wheat, as we know it, and the scourge that of the white weevil.

2. Oliver Evans, of Delaware, had invented machinery for moving grain and flour by a succession of elevators, conveyors, hopper boys, and descenders.

ᴈᴈ 1 8 0 2 ᴈᴈ

A Querulous Guest
from Washington

ANNA THORNTON was the wife of Dr. William Thornton, de-
signer of the United States Capitol and head of the Patent
Office in Washington. Escorted by James and Dolley Madison, the Thorntons, with her mother, arrived from Montpelier on a stormy evening in September 1802. The house was
full of guests, and Mrs. Thornton found little to please her.
On a second visit four years later she thought the house and
grounds were much improved. "It is quite a handsome place,"
she wrote. This account of her first visit is from Mrs. Thornton's diary.

SATURDAY 18th . . . About ½ after ten we all set out on our journey
to Monticello. Bishop M.[adison] accompanied us about 12 miles on
the way—it was very warm riding & the roads bad—we travelled so
slowly that it was quite dark before we reached the foot of the mountain and had it not been for the lightning was played almost inces-
santly we should not have been able to have seen the road at all; at
last, we became so much afraid that we alighted, and all but Mama
walked the remainder of the way to the house, which I suppose might
be about ¾ of a mile. The exercise of ascending the hill and the
warmth of the evening fatigued us much. I kept up my spirits so much
that by the time I got to my chamber I was exhausted & quite unwell.
Besides the darkness of the night, and the roads which lead thro'
woods principally, there was every appearance of a thunderstorm; fortunately we arrived safe about ¼ hour before it began to rain violently. Tho' I had been prepared to see an unfinished house, still I

could not help being much struck with the uncommon appearance &
which the general gloom that prevailed contributed much to increase.
We went thro' a large unfinished hall, loose plank forming the floor,
lighted by one dull lanthern, into a large room with a small bow and
separated by an arch, where the company were seated at tea. No light
being in the large part of the room & part of the family being seated
there, the appearance was irregular & unpleasant. When we went to
bed we had to mount a little ladder of a staircase about 2 feet wide
and very steep, into rooms with the beds fixed up in recesses in the
walls—the windows square and small turning in pivots. Everything
has a whimsical and droll appearance.

Sunday 19th—Upon examining the plan I find it within side that it
will be handsome & convenient. The president intends compleating it
next summer [but] he has altered his plan so frequently, pulled down
& rebuilt, that in many parts without side it looks like a house going
to decay from the length of time that it has been erected. At seven
o'clock the bell rang to announce that it was time to prepare for
breakfast, and in about another hour we were summoned. The party
consisted of the president, Mr. and Mrs. Randolph. Mr. and Mrs.
Eppes, daughters of Mr. Jefferson. Mr. Short lately from France, Mr.
R. Jefferson brother of the president, Miss Virginia Randolph sister to
Mr. Randolph, two Miss Browns and Miss House & Mr. Venables.
Judge Jones and Mr. Cabell came to dinner. Dinner at 5 o'clock—
announced us at Breakfast—no wine drank till the cloth is removed.
Dr. Bache came to visit as Mrs. Eppe's little son is very sick. Mrs.
Randolph has five very fine children, she is a very accomplished sen-
sible woman, and takes great pains to instruct them. She is not hand-
some. Mrs. Eppes is very beautiful but much more reserved than Mrs.
Randolph. They take it in turn to superintend the family when they
are with their father. They have homes which they go to when he is
absent from Monticello.

Monday 20th—Miss Browns & Miss House went home. Dr. and
Mrs. Bache came while we were at dinner. Mr. Clifton from Phila
dined here & staid all night. Dr. T & Miss Payne & I wrote a letter
together to Mrs. Forrest. Dr. T wrote to Mr. Latimer. The president's
bedchamber is only separated from the library by an arch; he keeps it
constantly locked, and I have been disappointed much by not being
able to get in to day.

Tuesday 21st—Mr. Thornton[1] arrived this morning, went into the Library which is very extensive, and said to be one of the best private Libraries on the continent. The president shewed some books of fine prints, particularly views of the ruins of [Baalbec]. Staid there till it was time to dress for dinner. Chess this Evening.

Wednesday 22.—Took a walk of half a mile which has been made round the Hill, thro the trees; below there is another of two miles. The grounds want a great deal of improvement yet, tho a great deal has been done. The House is situated on the very summit of the mountain, on a circular level, formed by art, commanding a view of all the surrounding country, the small town of Charlottesville, and a little winding river (called the Ravenna) with a view of the blue ridge & even more distant mountains form a beautiful scene on the north side of the house. There is something grand & awful in the situation but far from convenient or in my opinion agreeable. It is a place you wou'd rather look at now & then than live at. Mr. J. has been 27 years engaged in improving the place, but he has pulled down & built up again so often, that nothing is compleated, nor do I think ever will be. A great deal of money has been expended both above & below ground, but not so as to appear to the best advantage.

The president was very much engaged & interested in a phaeton which he had constructed after *eight years preparation.* The mind of the P. of the U.S. ought to have more important occupation. He is a very long time maturing his projects.

Diary, entries of Sept. 18–22, 1802, Papers of Mrs. William Thornton, Library of Congress.

1. Edward Thornton, British chargé d'affairs, also thought the house already in decay.

⚜ 1807 ⚜

The Visit of a British Diplomat

AUGUSTUS JOHN FOSTER was an aristocratic young English-man embarked on a career in the foreign service. Appointed secretary of the legation in Washington while Jefferson was president, he, like Anthony Merry, the British minister, had little affection for Jefferson or the United States, though he managed to conceal his contempt behind bland manners. He visited Monticello, after Montpelier, in August 1807. In 1811, after service in Stockholm, Foster returned to the United States as the last British minister before the war. Drawing upon notes collected during both tours of duty, Foster later wrote a narrative of his American experience. It was edited by Richard Beale Davis and published as *Jeffersonian America* in 1954. Most of Davis's notes have been omitted.

IT IS A VERY DELIGHTFUL ride of twenty-eight miles from Montpellier to . . . Mr. Jefferson's seat at Monticello, the road lying at the foot of the Southwest Ridge. There was a good tavern too by the way where I got a comfortable bed, the innkeeper being a Major Gordon who was also a farmer; and I passed a very pretty wooden house[1] with a portico belonging to a Mr. Walker at the halfway, as well as several other settlements—as farm houses on a large scale are called in these parts—on either side of the road. This is rather a populous district, besides that it is the great high road to New Orleans, to which the mail was carried in twenty days from Washington, and that it also leads to the different springs beyond the Blue Ridge, where there is a considerable resort of company in the hot season.

President Jefferson, when he withdrew, which he was in the habit of doing every month of August, to Monticello, for two months, in order to avoid the bad air of the city of Washington, had a daily mail sent to him on horseback from Fredericksburg by Mr. Madison's house. And there is a regular weekly stage coach which passed within two miles of his place and crossed the Blue Ridge at the Rock-fish Gap, so that living among these forests was far from being insulated from all intercourse with the great world. There was a disagreeable ford to cross at the North [Rivanna] River near Monticello which lamed one of my horses just as I was preparing to ascend. The mountain itself is separated from the range on either side and lies between two gaps. The ascent is very winding, about a mile in length and very well shaded until within about two hundred yards from the house which is built on a level platform that was formed by the President's father who cut down the top of the mount to the extent of about two acres.

The house has two porticoes of the Doric order, though one of them was not quite completed, and the pediment had in the meanwhile to be supported on the stems of four tulip trees, which are really, when well grown, as beautiful as the fluted shafts of Corinthian pillars. They front north and south. On the ground floor were four sitting rooms, two bed rooms and the library, which contained several thousand volumes classed according to subject and language. It was divided into three compartments, in one of which the President had his bed placed in a doorway. And in a recess at the foot of the bed was a horse with forty-eight projecting hands on which hung his coats and waistcoats and which he could turn round with a long stick, a knick-knack that Jefferson was fond of showing with many other little mechanical inventions. Another was a sulky upon four wheels with the spring in the centre, a very rough sort of carriage but which he preferred to any other as having been made by an Irish mechanic at Monticello under his own superintendence and to praise which was a sure way to prejudice him in your favour.

He had also got an odometer, made by a Mr. Clark, a man of good natural turn for mechanics, which was fastened upon the axle-tree of the sulky and would tell the number of miles gone over by the wheels. This, however, seemed a really useful invention and Mr. Clark, who had been in the habit of using it for twenty years, declared that it answered perfectly well. It was contained in a box and looked like a mariner's compass. A blade of iron, hooked at one end, projected from the box upon the box of the wheel, and the hooked part being moved upwards with the rotatory motion, each time this occurred, the blades of iron gave an impulse to an interior small wheel which again moved another that communicated with a hand like the hand of a dial, when this pointed to the number of miles marked, which altogether only amounted to ten. Every ten miles the machine striking like a clock, after which it goes its round again until a second ten miles are completed and so on in succession. Such an invention may easily be conceived to be of great use in a country like America where it would often be difficult in any other mode to ascertain the distances one travels over with any accuracy.

In Mr. Jefferson's library there was a picture representing a battle, painted by one of the Big-bellied tribe of Indians, who live upon the Missouri, on a buffalo hide, very grotesque, as may be supposed, but extremely interesting. It represents several Indians in single combat, with tomahawks or spears and shields, fighting on horseback. Where a white man was intended to be represented he is painted with the accompaniments of a gun and cocked hat. The whole is rudely sketched, and the men seem sliding off instead of sitting on their horses. There is another painting of the same kind in the hall of the house but this latter is not as well executed as the first. There is also a map of a part of the Missouri, together with a couple of stone idols in a sitting posture.

Among the most interesting of the President's books was one which had been published in the year 1776 by the Archbishop of Toledo,[2] but was afterwards suppressed by order of the Spanish government before many copies of it could have got into circulation. It had been, however, printed at Mexico, and contained prints representing the habiliments of war and peace of the Mexicans, and the great temple at Mexico, besides Cortes' letters and many curious details relative to the conquest by the Spaniards, and to Indian customs. Heriot's collection of voyages among the Indians in three folio volumes was also lying on the table.[3] Heriot was a servant of Sir Walter Raleigh, and Captain [Meriwether] Lewis, previously to my looking into this book, had given me an account of many usages as existing at the present day, which are described by Heriot as then peculiar to the Indians whom he visited, those described by Lewis being settled on the banks of the

Missouri. If the library had been thrown open to guests, the President's country house would have been as agreeable a place to stay at as any I know, but it was there he sat and wrote and he did not like of course to be disturbed by visitors who in this part of the world are rather disposed to be indiscreet.

The family breakfast hour was eight o'clock. After breakfast Mrs. Randolph and her amiable daughters as well as the other female relations of the house set about cleaning the tea things and washing the alabaster lamp, which I took to be designed as a catch for popularity. After this operation the President retired to his books, his daughter to give lessons to her children, her husband to his farm, and the guests were left to amuse themselves as they pleased till four o'clock, walking, riding or shooting. The President took his daily ride at one o'clock to look at his farm and mill, at four dinner was served up and in the evening we walked on a wooden terrace or strolled into the wood, Mr. Jefferson playing with his grandchildren till dusk when tea was brought in, and afterward wine and fruit of which the peaches were excellent. At nine o'clock our host withdrew and everybody else as they pleased. Mr. Randolph's son,[4] a youth of sixteen, who was at school at the village of Milton close by, generally came in the evening. He was a fine young lad, and, according to what I was told was a general custom in Virginia among boys, he walked into the drawing room, without shoes or stockings, tho' very neatly dressed in other respects. I had, however, reason to doubt afterwards that the practice was so general and I believe it was a mere whim of his grandfather, who in the very first conversation I had with him expressed his wonder that feet were not as often washed as hands and would I dare say, if he could have ventured it without ridicule, have been for a still greater degree of nakedness, so fond was he of leaving nature as unconfined as possible in all her works.

The President was considered a very bad farmer. He had some excellent red land, however, about Monticello and a profitable estate in the county of Bedford about ninety miles from thence, but his estate suffered prodigiously from the tendency of the soil to gully, which cannot well be prevented on hilly ground, and is very much promoted by the culture of Indian corn. The slightest track opens the way for a gully, and that of a plough-share dragged negligently through a field may be the commencement of a chasm in which houses afterwards might be buried. One side of the hill on which Monticello stands has been so disfigured in this way that they have been obliged to scatter Scotch Broom seed over it, which at last succeeded in, at least, hiding the cavities. Tobacco is the most profitable produce of the soil, and next to it, Indian corn of which I have been told some land belonging to Mr. Garnet, on the Rappahannock, will yield forty-eight bushels to the acre.

Mr. Jefferson told me that in the year 1791 there were about 292,500 slaves in Virginia, the whole number of the inhabitants of the state being at that time but 747,500. And of those 292,500, nearly 200,000 were to be found in the forty-four counties along the Chesapeake Bay with the great rivers which fall into it, while the free persons in those counties amounted to but 198,000. About the same period there were but 700,000 slaves in the whole of the United States, of which number above 630,000 were living in the states south of the Delaware. The price of a slave on an average was about $400, and the President said he thought that they increased in population more rapidly than the whites.

Their oaths were valid against one another but not against a white man; neither was the oath of a free Negro allowed to be valid against white people. Free Negroes associated and intermarried with slaves, but the slaves of a proprietor who was master of 500 or 600 of them considered themselves as vastly superior to those of a man who owned but two or three. Mr. Jefferson told me of a Negro named Bannister,[5] who died in the year 1806, at Baltimore, being a perfect black, the son of an African, and who had acquired considerable knowledge in mathematics so as to be able to solve very difficult problems. He annually published an almanac but the President asserted that in other respects he appeared to little advantage, particularly in his letters, he having received several from him which were very childish and trivial. He told me, also, that the Negroes have, in general, so little foresight that though they receive blankets very thankfully from their masters on the commencement of winter and use them to keep off the cold, yet when the warm weather returns they will frequently cast them off, without a thought as to what may become of them, wherever they may happen to be at the time, and then not seldom lose them in the woods or the fields from mere carelessness.

Jefferson's opinions in regard to the mental qualities of the Negro race were certainly not favourable. . . .[6]

He was happy enough to have his daughters both married in Virginia, one to Mr. Thomas Mann Randolph, a gentleman of property and who claimed to descend on the mother's side from the Indian queen, Pocahontas, as his cousin John Randolph claimed to be descended from her by the father's side. The other daughter was married to Mr. Eppes. Both gentlemen were Members of Congress and both were planters, as indeed more than two-thirds of the deputies are who represent this aristocratic state, which has taken the lead of all the states in preaching ultra democratical principles and in governing the Union by means of its gentleman Jacobins, who were not to be had in such numbers nor of such abilities from any other part of the continent. Mr. Jefferson was in frequent correspondence with Madame de Staël and when I visited him he had just received *Corinne* from her, with a letter in which, he observed, she had written strong things in little space. She told him that there was not but one man [Napoleon] in Europe, that she was not allowed by him to live in Paris, but at a small distance from it, and that every day there came to visit her Volney, Dupont, several conservative Senators and others who were still warm Republicans though they kissed the rod.

He, Jefferson, speculated on what would be the fate of France in the event of Bonaparte's death and said he was of opinion they would agree to be under any monarch rather than hazard another revolution of a Jacobinical description. In speaking of Talleyrand he told me that he had always, while in the United States, affected to be ignorant of the English language, but that when walking one day with General Dearborn, he forgot himself and came out with a question in English about some indifferent matter, and at Paris, after his return from America, though he conversed with General Armstrong, the American envoy, in English to Mr. Fox and other British persons, he pretended not to know it. Mr. Jefferson had been in the south of France and said those meridional provinces would have made a fine flourishing state, on which I observed how near they were to being rendered a separate country by the Revolution, and he added he wished they had been so separated, for that if France, like North America, had been divided into small states they would not have troubled their neighbours so much.

Mr. Jefferson in speaking of the Brazils, surprized me by his ideas regarding that country, as he maintained that the United States would have to supply them with provisions, and that it had never been able to supply Portugal. Tho' when I observed that there was great variety of soil in it fit for anything, he admitted the fact, and said that he was convinced they might even make wine in some of the provinces. I ventured to ask if he intended to open diplomatic relations with the Court of Rio Janeiro but he told me he expected they would announce themselves, as in general it was the custom for strangers to make the first visit tho' it was true the contrary custom was that which prevailed in the United States. . . .

I thought Mr. Jefferson more of a statesman and man of the world than Mr. Madison, who was rather too much of the disputatious pleader. Yet the latter, however, was better informed, and, moreover, was a social, jovial and good-humored companion full of anecdote and sometimes matter of a loose description relating to old times, but oftener of a political and historical interest. During the time when Congress sat at Philadelphia he fell in love with Mrs. Todd, who presided at the boarding house where he lived, and married her. She must have been a very handsome woman and tho' an uncultivated mind and fond of gossiping, was so perfectly good-tempered and good-humoured that she rendered her husband's house as far as depended on her agreeable to all parties.

Mr. Madison was a little man, with small features rather wizened when I saw him, but occasionally lit up with a good-natured smile. He wore a black coat, stockings with shoes buckled, and had his hair powdered, with a tail. Jefferson on the other hand was, as before stated, very tall and bony and affected to despise dress. In conversation too he was visionary and loved to dream, eyes open, or, as the Germans say, "zu schwärmen," and it must be owned that America is the paradise for "Schwärmers," futurity there offering a wide frame for all that the imagination can put into it. If he lived, however, on illusions and mystic philanthropical plans for the benefit of mankind in the country, or in his bed, he was not the less awake or active in taking measures to ensure the triumph of himself and his party at the capital of the Union, and I doubt if General Washington himself would so certainly have been elected for the third time to the presidential chair as he would have been, had he chosen to be put into nomination for it. But he preferred being consistent and to follow in this respect the example of his great predecessor, while he had enough of independence of mind and love for even trifling occupations to enable him to bear the change with composure. . . .

At Monticello I was present at some of the national sports and games, of which there are more in Virginia than in any other state that I have visited. Horse racing is carried very far and gives rise to a good deal of gambling. Cock-fighting is on the decline, but still exists here and there. Quoits and nine-pins are much in fashion. And as to festivities they are, especially the barbecues, most numerously attended on the Atlantic side of the Blue Ridge. A barbecue originally was a meeting in the woods to partake of a pig roasted whole. A pit was dug in the ground, fire placed in it, and a large pig supported on four stakes was put over the fire. There is always a dance afterward, and I was told that at some places these meetings are exceedingly numerous, even the better sort of people attending them. Barbecues are now oftener held at a tavern and are very frequent during summer. People think nothing of going ten to twelve miles to one.

On the other side of the Blue Ridge, which is near 4,000 feet above the level of the sea, and which I crossed at Rock-fish Gap by a stony winding road, the people differ very much in their habits and manners from Virginians of the plain. They even affect to give themselves and the others distinguishing epithets which, though now called nicknames, may in time become national denominations. They call themselves Cohees tho' from their accent in many places one should guess them to be Highlanders. And their neighbours they call the Old Virginians or the Tuckahoe people, both being terms which are probably derived from the names of extinct Indian tribes. However that may be, I was certainly struck with the more active healthy appearance of the Cohees and were I to become a settler in this part of the world I should, I think, prefer their district to that of the Tuckahoes, tho' there is a great deal to say upon the advantages of being located near a great town and though the American mountaineer is after all but a rough unfashioned kind of being.

From Monticello I proceeded to the Natural Bridge, and rode through beautiful woods which were full of wild turkeys that I in vain endeavoured to put up, they so much preferred running and were so very swift of foot.

Jeffersonian America: Notes on the United States of America Collected in the Years 1805–6–7 and 11–12 by Sir Augustus Foster, Bart., ed. Richard Beale Davis (San Marino, Calif., 1954), 143–49,

153–56, 160–61. Reprinted by permission of the Henry E. Huntington Library and Art Gallery.

1. Castle Hill.

2. Davis's note: Foster's date may be 1770. At any rate, he refers to *Historia de Nueva-España por su Esclarecido Conquistador Hernan Cortes, aumentada con otros Documentos, y Notas, por el Illustrissimo Señor Don Francisco Antonio Lorenzana, Arzobispo de Mexico* . . . , Ano de 1770.

3. Davis's note: The Theodor de Bry edition of Thomas Harriot's *Briefe and true report of the new found land of Virginia* . . . , Parts I, II, and III (Frankfurt, 1590, 1591, 1592, etc.).

4. Thomas Jefferson Randolph.

5. Benjamin Banneker.

6. Jefferson had expressed his opinion of the Negro in Query XIV of *Notes on Virginia,* an opinion he later modified somewhat.

⌐⊀ 1809 ⊁⌐

)

"The Haven of Domestic Life"

PROBABLY THE MOST CHARMING of all the visitors' accounts is that of Margaret Bayard Smith. The daughter of a leading Federalist family in Philadelphia, she married Samuel Harrison Smith, a Republican newspaper editor, who whisked her to the new capital on the Potomac, Washington, where he established the Republican press, *The National Intelligencer,* under Jefferson's patronage in 1800. When Jefferson became president, the Smiths were frequent guests at the White House. Mrs. Smith quickly shed her Federalist prejudices and became an adoring friend. Her description of the family's visit to Monticello just four months after Jefferson's retirement, at age sixty-six, is especially valuable for the happy picture it paints of him in the midst of domestic life. The account is based upon Mrs. Smith's notes and letters, from which Gaillard Hunt edited *The First Forty Years of Washington Society* in 1906.

AFTER A VERY DELIGHTFUL journey of three days, we reached Monticello on the morning of the fourth. When I crossed the Ravanna, a wild and romantic little river, which flows at the foot of the mountain, my heart beat,—I thought I had entered, as it were the threshold of his dwelling, and I looked around everywhere expecting to meet with some trace of his superintending care. In this I was disappointed, for no vestige of the labour of man appeared; nature seemed to hold an undisturbed dominion. We began to ascend this mountain, still as we rose I cast my eyes around, but could discern nothing but untamed

45

woodland, after a mile's winding upwards, we saw a field of corn, but the road was still wild and uncultivated. I every moment expected to reach the summit, and felt as if it was an endless road; my impatience lengthened it, for it is not two miles from the outer gate on the river to the house. At last we reached the summit, and I shall never forget the emotion the first view of this sublime scenery excited. Below me extended for above 60 miles round, a country covered with woods, plantations and houses; beyond, arose the blue mountains, in all their grandeur. Monticello rising 500 feet above the river, of a conical form and standing by itself, commands on all sides an unobstructed and I suppose one of the most extensive views any spot [on] the globe affords. The sides of the mountain covered with wood, scarcely a speck of cultivation, present a fine contrast to its summit, crowned with a noble pile of buildings, surrounded by an immense lawn, and shaded here and there with some fine trees. Before we reached the house, we met Mr. J. on horseback, he had just returned from his morning ride, and when, on approaching, he recognized us, he received us with one of those benignant smiles, and cordial tones of voice that convey an undoubted welcome to the heart. He dismounted and assisted me from the carriage, led us to the hall thro' a noble portico, where he again bade us welcome. I was so struck with the appearance of this Hall, that I lingered to look around, but he led me forward, smiling as he said, "You shall look bye and bye, but you must now rest." Leading me to a sopha in a drawing room as singular and beautiful as the Hall, he rang and sent word to Mrs. Randolph that we were there, and then ordered some refreshments. "We have quite a sick family," said he; "My daughter has been confined to the sick bed of her little son; my grand-daughter has already lost her's and still keeps to her room and several of the younger children are indisposed. For a fortnight Mr. and Mrs. Randolph have sat up every night, until they are almost worn out." This information clouded my satisfaction and cast a gloom over our visit,—but Mrs. R. soon entered, and with a smiling face, most affectionately welcomed us. Her kind and cheerful manners soon dispersed my gloom and after a little chat, I begged her not to let me detain her from her nursery, but to allow me to follow her to it; she assented and I sat with her until dinner time. Anne, (Mrs. Bankhead) who had been confined 3 weeks before and had lost her child looked delicate and interesting; Ellen, my old favorite, I found improved as well as grown. At five o'clock the bell summoned us to dinner. Mr. Randolph, Mr. Bankhead, and Jefferson R. were there. They are 12 in family, and as Mr. J. sat in the midst of his children and grand-children, I looked on him with emotions of tenderness and respect. The table was plainly, but genteely and plentifully spread, and his immense and costly variety of French and Italian wines, gave place to Madeira and a sweet ladies' wine. We sat till near sun down at the table, where the dessert was succeeded by agreeable and instructive conversation in which every one seemed to wish and expect Mr. J. to take the chief part. As it is his custom after breakfast to withdraw to his own apartments and pursuits and not to join the family again until dinner, he prolongs that meal, or rather the time after that meal, and seems to relish his wine the better for being accompanied with conversation, and during the four days I spent there these were the most social hours. When he rose from the table, a walk was proposed and he accompanied us. He took us to the garden he has commenced since his retirement. It is on the south side of the mountain and commands a most noble view. Little is as yet done. A terrace of 70 or 80 feet long and about 40 feet wide is already made and in cultivation. A broad grass walk leads along the outer edge; the inner part is laid off in beds for vegetables. This terrace is to be extended in length and another to be made below it. The view it commands, is at present its greatest beauty. We afterwards walked round the first circuit. There are 4 roads about 15 or 20 feet wide, cut round the mountain from 100 to 200 feet apart. These circuits are connected by a great many roads and paths and when completed will afford a beautiful shady ride or walk of seven miles. The first circuit is not quite a mile round, as it is near the very top. It is in general shady, with openings through the trees for distant views. We passed the outhouses for slaves and workmen. They are all much better than I have seen on any other plantation, but to an eye unaccustomed to such sights, they appear poor and their cabins form a most unpleasant contrast with the place that rises so near them. Mr. J. has carpenters, cabinet-makers, painters, and blacksmiths and several other trades all within himself, and finds these slaves excellent workmen. As we walked, he explained his future designs. "My long absence from this place, has left a wilderness around me." "But you have returned," said I, "and the wilderness shall blossom like the rose and you, I hope, will long sit beneath your own vine

47

and your own fig-tree." It was near dark when we reached the house; he led us into a little tea room which opened on the terrace and as Mrs. R. was still in her nursery he sat with us and conversed until tea time. We never drank tea until near nine, afterwards there was fruit, which he seldom staid to partake of, as he always retired immediately after tea. I never sat above an hour afterwards, as I supposed Mrs. R. must wish to be in her nursery. I rose the morning after my arrival very early and went out on the terrace, to contemplate scenery, which to me was so novel. The space between Monticello and the Allegany, from sixty to eighty miles, was covered with a thick fog, which had the appearance of the ocean and was unbroken except when wood covered hills rose above the plain and looked like islands. As the sun rose, the fog was broken and exhibited the most various and fantastic forms, lakes, rivers, bays, and as it ascended, it hung in white fleecy clouds on the sides of the mountain; an hour afterwards you would scarcely believe it was the same scene you looked on. In spite of the cold air from the mountains, I staid there until the first breakfast bell rang. Our breakfast table was as large as our dinner table; instead of a cloth a folded napkin lay under each plate; we had tea, coffee, excellent muffins, hot wheat and corn bread, cold ham and butter. It was not exactly the Virginia breakfast I expected. Here indeed was the mode of living in general that of a Virginia planter. At breakfast the family all assembled, all Mrs. R's. children eat at the family table, but are in such excellent order, that you would not know, if you did not see them, that a child was present. After breakfast, I soon learned that it was the habit of the family each separately to pursue their occupations. Mr. J. went to his apartments, the door of which is never opened but by himself and his retirement seems so sacred that I told him it was his sanctum sanctorum. Mr. Randolph rides over to his farm and seldom returns until night; Mr. Bankhead who is reading law to his study; a small building at the end of the east terrace, opposite to Mr. Randolph's which terminates the west terrace; these buildings are called pavilions. Jefferson R. went to survey a tract of woodland, afterwards make[s] his report to his grand father. Mrs. Randolph withdrew to her nursery and excepting the hours housekeeping requires she devotes the rest to her children, whom she instructs. As for them, they seem never to leave her for an instant, but are always beside her or on her lap.

48

Visitors generally retire to their own rooms, or walk about the place; those who are fond of reading can never be at a loss, those who are not will some times feel wearied in the long interval between breakfast and dinner. The dinner bell rings twice, the first collects the family in time to enter the room by the time the second announces dinner to be on the table, which while I was there was between 4 and 5 o'clock. In summer the interval between rising from table and tea (9 o'clock) may be agreeably passed in walking. But to return to my journal. After breakfast on Sunday morning, I asked Ellen to go with me on the top of the house; Mr. J. heard me and went along with us and pointed out those spots in the landscape most remarkable. The morning was show'ry, the clouds had a fine effect, throwing large masses of shade on the mountain sides, which finely contrasted with the sunshine of other spots. He afterwards took us to the drawing room, 26 or 7 feet diameter, in the dome. It is a noble and beautiful apartment, with 8 circular windows and a sky-light. It was not furnished and being in the attic story is not used, which I thought a great pity, as it might be made the most beautiful room in the house. The attic chambers are comfortable and neatly finished but no elegance. When we descended to the hall, he asked us to pass into the Library, or as I called it his sanctum sanctorum, where any other feet than his own seldom intrude. This suit of apartments opens from the Hall to the south. It consists of 3 rooms for the library, one for his cabinet, one for his chamber, and a green house divided from the other by glass compartments and doors; so that the view of the plants it contains, is unobstructed. He has not yet made his collection, having but just finished one room, which opens on one of the terraces. He showed us everything he thought would please or interest us. His most valuable and curious books—those which contained fine prints etc.—among these I thought the most curious were the original letters of Cortez to the King of Spain, a vol of fine views of ancient villas around Rome, with maps of the grounds, and minute descriptions of the buildings and grounds, an old poem written by Piers Plowman and printed 250 years ago; he read near a page, which was almost as unintelligible as if it was Hebrew; and some Greek romances. He took pains to find one that was translated into French, as most of them were translated in Latin and Italian. More than two hours passed most charmingly away. The library consists of books in all languages, and contains about twenty thousand vols,[1] but so disposed that they do not give the idea of a great library. I own I was much disappointed in its appearance, and I do not think with its numerous divisions and arches it is as impressive as one large room would have been. His cabinet and chamber contained every convenience and comfort, but were plain. His bed is built in the wall which divides his chamber and cabinet. He opened a little closet which contains all his garden seeds. They are all in little phials, labeled and hung on little hooks. Seeds such as peas, beans, etc. were in tin cannisters, but everything labeled and in the neatest order. He bade us take whatever books we wished, which we did, and then retired to our own room. Here we amused ourselves until dinner time excepting an hour I sat with Mrs. R. by her sick baby, but as she was reading I did not sit long. After dinner Ellen and Mr. Bankhead accompanied us in a long ramble in the mountain walks. At dark when we returned, the tea room was still vacant; I called Virginia and Mary (the age of my Julia and Susan) amused myself with them until their grand papa entered, with whom I had a long and interesting conversation; in which he described with enthusiasm his retirement from public life and the pleasure he found in domestic.

Monday morning. I again rose early in order to observe the scenes around me and was again repaid for the loss of sleep, by the various appearances the landscape assumed as the fog was rising. But the blue and misty mountains, now lighted up with sunshine, now thrown into deep shadow, presented objects on which I gaze each morning with new pleasure. After breakfast Mr J. sent E. to me to ask if I would take a ride with him round the mountain; I willingly assented and in a little while I was summoned; the carriage was a kind of chair which his own workmen had made under his direction, and it was with difficulty that he, Ellen and I found room in it, and might well be called the sociable. The first circuit, the road was good, and I enjoyed the views it afforded and the familiar and easy conversation, which our sociable gave rise to; but when we descended to the second and third circuit, fear took from me the power of listening to him, or observing the scene, nor could I forbear expressing my alarm, as we went along a rough road which had only been laid out, and on driving over fallen trees, and great rocks, which threatened an overset to our sociable and a roll down the mountains to us. "My dear madam," said Mr. J., "you are not to be afraid, or if you are you are not to show it; trust yourself implicitly to me, I will answer for your safety; I came every foot of this road yesterday, on purpose to see if a carriage could come safely; I know every step I take, so banish all fear." This I tried to do, but in vain, till coming to a road over which one wheel must pass I jumped out, while the servant who attended on horseback rode forward and held up the carriage as Mr. J. passed. Poor Ellen did not dare to get out. Notwithstanding the terror I suffered I would not have lost this ride; as Mr. J. explained to me all his plans for improvement, where the roads, the walks, the seats, the little temples were to be placed. There are two springs gushing from the mountain side; he took me to one which might be made very picturesque. As we passed the grave-yard, which is about half way down the mountain, in a sequestered spot, he told me he there meant to place a small gothic building,—higher up, where a beautiful little mound was covered with a grove of trees, he meant to place a monument to his friend [George] Wythe. We returned home by a road which did not wind round the mountain but carried us to the summit by a gentle ascent. It was a good road, and my terror vanished and I enjoyed conversation. I found Mrs. R. deeply engaged in the Wild Irish Boy[2] sitting by the side of her little patient; I did not stay long to interrupt her, but finding Mrs. Bankhead likewise engaged with a book, I withdrew to my own room to read my Grecian romance. At dinner Mrs. Randolph sent an apology, she hurt her eye so badly, that it produced excessive inflammation and pain, which obliged her to go to bed. After dinner I went up to sit by her, Mr. J. came up soon after and I was delighted by his tender attentions to their dear daughter. As he sat by her and held her hand, for above an hour, we had a long social conversation in which Mrs. R. joined in occasionally. After he had gone, finding her disposed to sleep, I went down. It was now quite dark and too late to walk, so I took my seat in the tea room with my little girls and told them stories till the tea bell again collected the family.

Tuesday. After breakfast I went up and sat all the morning by Mrs. Randolph; she was too unwell to rise; part of the time I read, but when we were alone, conversed. Our conversation turned chiefly on her father, and on her mentioning their correspondence, I begged her to show me some of his letters. This she willingly assented to and it was a rich repast to mind and heart. Some of them were written when he was minister in France and she in a convent. These are filled with the best advice in the best language. His letters come down to the last days of his political life; in every one he expresses his longings after retirement. She was so good as to give me one of these precious letters. When I went down stairs I found Mr. J. in the hall and Mr. S[mith], and we had a long conversation on a variety of topics. He took us a charming walk round the edge of the lawn and showed us the spots from which the house appeared to most advantage. I looked upon him as he walked, the top of this mountain, as a being elevated above the mass of mankind, as much in character as he was in local situation. I reflected on the long career of public duties and stations through which he had passed, and that after forty years spent on the tempestuous sea of political life, he had now reached the haven of domestic life. Here while the storm roared at a distance, he could hear its roaring and be at peace. He had been a faithful labourer in the harvest field of life, his labours were crowned with success, and he had reaped a rich harvest of fame and wealth and honor. All that in this, his winter of life he may enjoy the harvest he has reaped. In him I perceive no decay of mind or debility of frame and to all the wisdom and experience of age, he adds the enthusiasm and ardour of youth. I looked on him with wonder as I heard him describe the improvements he designed in his grounds, they seemed to require a whole life to carry into effect, and a young man might doubt of ever completing or enjoying them. But he seems to have transposed his hopes and anticipations into the existence of his children. It is in them he lives, and I believe he finds as much delight in the idea that they will enjoy the fruit of his present labours, as if he hoped it for himself. If full occupation of mind, heart and hands, is happiness, surely he is happy. The sun never sees him in bed, and his mind designs more than the day can fulfill, even his long day. The conversation of the morning, the letters I had read, and the idea that this was the last day I was to spend in his society, the last time I was ever to see him, filled my heart with sadness. I could scarcely look at or speak to him without tears. After dinner he went to the carpenter's shop, to give directions for a walking seat he had ordered made for us, and I did not see him again until after sun-set. I spent the interval walking with Mr. Smith round the lawn and grave, and had just parted from him to join the children to whom I had promised another story, when as I passed the terrace, Mr.

J. came out and joined us. The children ran to him and immediately proposed a race; we seated ourselves on the steps of the Portico, and he after placing the children according to their size one before the other, gave the word for starting and away they flew; the course round this back lawn was a qr. of a mile, the little girls were much tired by the time they returned to the spot from which they started and came panting and out of breath to throw themselves into their grandfather's arms, which were opened to receive them; he pressed them to his bosom and rewarded them with a kiss; he was sitting on the grass and they sat down by him, until they were rested; then they again wished to set off; he thought it too long a course for little Mary and proposed running on the terrace. Thither we went, and seating ourselves at one end, they ran from us to the pavilion and back again; "What an amusement," said I, "do these little creatures afford us." "Yes," replied he, "it is only with them that a grave man can play the fool." They now called on him to run with them, he did not long resist and seemed delighted in delighting them. Oh ye whose envenomed calumny has painted him as the slave of the vilest passions, come here and contemplate this scene! The simplicity, the gaiety, the modesty and gentleness of a child, united to all that is great and venerable in the human character. His life is the best refutation of the calumnies that have been heaped upon him and it seems to me impossible, for any one personally to know him and remain his enemy. It was dark by the time we entered the tearoom. I was glad to close the windows and shut out the keen air from the mountains. The mornings and evenings are here always cool and indeed Mrs. Randolph says it is never hot. As it was the last evening we were to pass here, Mr. J. sat longer than usual after tea. . . .

After tea, fruit as usual was brought, of which he staid to partake; the figs were very fine and I eat them with greater pleasure from their having been planted rear'd and attended by him with peculiar care, which this year was rewarded with an abundant crop, and of which we every day enjoyed the produce.

Wednesday morning. Mrs. Randolph was not able to come down to breakfast, and I felt too sad to join in the conversation. I looked on every object around me, all was examined with that attention a last look inspires; the breakfast ended, our carriage was at the door, and I rose to bid farewell to this interesting family. Mrs. R. came down to spend the last minutes with us. As I stood for a moment in the Hall, Mr. J. approached and in the most cordial manner urged me to make another visit the ensuing summer, I told him with a voice almost choked with tears, "that I had no hope of such a pleasure—this," said I, raising my eyes to him, "is the last time I fear in this world at least, that I shall ever see you—But there is another world." I felt so affected by the idea of this last sight of this good and great man, that I turned away and hastily repeating my farewell to the family, gave him my hand, he pressed it affectionately as he put me in the carriage saying, "God bless you, dear madam. God bless you." "And God bless you," said I, from the very bottom of my heart.

Mr. Smith got in, the door shut and we drove from the habitation of philosophy and virtue. How rapidly did we seem to descend that mountain which had seemed so tedious in its ascent, and the quick pulsations I then felt were now changed to a heavy oppression.

Margaret Bayard Smith, *The First Forty Years of Washington Society,* ed. Galliard Hunt (New York, 1906), 66–79.

1. A more accurate estimate would be seven thousand volumes.

2. Probably a ballad or story.

7

Boston Comes
to Monticello

THIS AND THE NEXT selection are complementary. Francis
Calley Gray, Massachusetts born and Harvard educated, was
only twenty-four years of age when he and his friend George
Ticknor made a tour of the Mid-Atlantic states that took
them as far south as Monticello in 1814–15. Gray had been
John Quincy Adams's secretary in the legation at St. Petersburg; he and Ticknor carried letters of introduction from
John Adams, with whom Jefferson had resumed a long-
interrupted correspondence. A winter journey to Monticello,
as Gray's journal attests, was not for the weak or faint-
hearted. His account—Ticknor's as well—is especially valuable for the glimpse it provides of Jefferson's great library just
after it had been sold to the United States but before it was
shipped to Washington to become the foundation of the Library of Congress. The journal was first published in 1924
with introduction and notes by Henry S. Rowe and T. Jefferson Coolidge, Jr., which are omitted here.

ON THURSDAY THE 2nd of February, Mr. Ticknor and myself at half
after three o'clock A.M. with each a small bundle left Richmond in the
stage coach for Charlottesville in the County of Albermarle, in order
to pay a visit to Mr. Jefferson, to whom we both had letters from Mr.
Adams. At twelve miles from town we passed Tuckahoe Creek and
soon after reached our breakfasting house, where, for the first time in
my life, I sat down to table with the landlord and his wife, and we
continued to do so during the whole ride to Charlotte. We were here

told that all the people east of the mountains call those on the west [side] cohees, and are called by them Tuckahoes. The first is Irish, from which nation the valley was first settled, and the latter the Indian name of a vegetable growing in the southern and eastern parts of Virginia eaten by the hogs and perhaps formerly by the inhabitants. (This vegetable I once supposed to be the truffle, but find from Mr. Jefferson that it certainly is not so.)

On leaving our breakfasting house we rode for sixteen miles through a fine country along the northern bank of [the] James River, soon quitting the country of coal in the centre of which is situated the inn at which we had breakfasted fourteen miles from Richmond. In several of the houses at which we stopped the whiskey drunk by the passengers did not form an item in the bill as they were private not public houses, i.e. they had no license.

At forty-five miles from Richmond according to the regular course of the stage we slept the first night. On the next day we passed through a miserable barren country covered with pines and found a ford at Junk Creek half frozen over and in quite as bad a state as the Matawoman. But our white driver with a spirit and industry far superior to that of the Maryland black, broke the ice before his horses and carried them through without difficulty. (A dead horse was lying on the farther bank, who had been drowned in attempting to pass). We overtook, particularly on the first day, many soldiers of the militia who had been in the service of the United States six months at Norfolk without winter clothing, exposed to three epidemics which desolated their camp, the ague and fever, the typhus, and the throat distemper, and were now discharged without pay. Many of them had not sufficient money to procure food and some, as we were told, had eaten nothing for thirty hours. The country constantly ascended as we proceeded west and on Friday soon after noon, we crossed the North River at the Ford near Milton and soon reached Monticello, between which and another mountain belonging to Mr. Jefferson, passed our road to Charlottesville, at which town we dined. It contains a few brick houses, a court house very large and a stone gaol, the basement story of which is occupied as shops by a couple of saddlers. This town, though the largest in this part of the country, contains no meeting-house, nor is there any within seven miles, but divine service is performed here in the court house every other Sunday. On Saturday it rained and at twelve o'clock we went from our tavern in a hack to Monticello, three miles east of Charlottesville on the same road we had passed the day before. Our road passed between Monticello and the S.W. mountain which is much higher and along whose side runs the narrow path which led us between these hills to the gate on the S.E. side of Monticello. The sides of both these hills and the valley between them are covered with a noble forest of oaks in all stages of growth and of decay. Their trunks straight and tall put forth no branches till they reach a height almost equal to the summits of our loftiest trees in New England. Those which were rooted in the valley, in the richest soil over-topped many which sprung from spots far above them on the side of the mountain. The forest had evidently been abandoned to nature; some of the trees were decaying from age, some were blasted, some uprooted by the wind and some appeared even to have been twisted from their trunks by the violence of a hurricane. They rendered the approach to the house even at this season of the year extremely grand and imposing. On reaching the house we found no bell nor knocker and, entering through the hall in the parlour, saw a gentleman (Col. Randolph), who took our letters to Mr. Jefferson.

Mr. Jefferson soon made his appearance. He is quite tall, six feet, one or two inches, face streaked and speckled with red, light grey eyes, white hair, dressed in shoes of very thin soft leather with pointed toes and heels ascending a peak behind, with very short quarters, grey worsted stockings, corduroy small clothes, blue waistcoat and coat, of stiff thick cloth made of the wool of his own merinoes and badly manufactured, the buttons of his coat and small clothes of horn, and an under waistcoat flannel bound with red velvet. His figure bony, long and with broad shoulders, a true Virginian. He begged he might put up our carriage, send for our baggage and keep us with him some time. We assented and he left the room to give the necessary directions, sending as we requested the carriage back to Charlottesville. On looking round the room in which we sat[1] the first thing which attracted our attention was the state of the chairs. They had leather bottoms stuffed with hair, but the bottoms were completely worn through and the hair sticking out in all directions; on the mantle-piece which was large and of marble were many books of all kinds, Livy, Orosius, Edinburg Review, 1 vol. of Edgeworth's Moral Tales, etc., etc. There were many miserable prints and some fine pictures hung round the room, among them two plans for the completion of the Capitol at Washington, one of them very elegant. A harpsichord stood in one corner of the room. There were four double windows from the wall to the floor of fine large glass and a recess in one side of the apartment. This was the breakfasting room. After half an hour's conversation with Mr. Jefferson and Col. Randolph, we were invited into the parlour where a fire was just kindled and a servant occupied in substituting a wooden panel for a square of glass, which had been broken in one of the folding doors opening on the lawn. Mr. Jefferson had procured the glass for his house in Bohemia, where the price is so much the square foot whatever be the size of the glass purchased, and these panes were so large that, unable to replace the square in this part of the country, he had been obliged to send to Boston to have some glass made of sufficient size to replace that broken, and this had not yet been received.

We passed the whole forenoon, which was rainy, in conversation with Mr. Jefferson and Mr. Randolph and at four o'clock toddy was brought us, which neither of us took, and which was never after handed again, and we were ushered back into the breakfast room to dinner, where we were introduced to Mrs. Randolph, Miss Randolph, and Mr. T. J. Randolph. The rest of the family at table were Mrs. Marks, a sister of Mr. Jefferson and two other daughters of Col. Randolph.

The drinking cups were of silver marked G.W. to T.J., the table liquors were beer and cider and after dinner wine. In the same room we took tea and at ten in the evening retired. Fires were lighted in our bedrooms and again in the morning before we rose and the beds were all in recesses.

At fifteen minutes after eight we heard the first breakfast bell and at nine, the second, whose sound assembled us in the breakfast room. We sat an hour after breakfast chating with the ladies and then adjourned to the parlour. Mr. Jefferson gave us the catalogue of his books to examine and soon after conducted us to his library, and passed an hour there in pointing out to us its principal treasures. His collection of ancient classics was complete as to the authors, but very careless in the editions. They were generally interleaved with the best English Translations. The Ancient English authors were also all here and some very rare editions of them. A black letter Chaucer and the first of Milton's Paradise Lost, divided into ten books, were the most remarkable. A considerable number of books valuable to the Biblical critic were here, and various ancient editions of all the genuine and apocryphal books, Erasmus' edition, etc. Many of the most valuable works on the civil and maritime law and on diplomacy, together with a complete collection of the laws of the different states, those of Virginia in manuscript, and all the old elementary writers and reporters of England formed the legal library. The ancient and most distinguished modern historians render this department nearly complete, and the histories and descriptions of the Kingdoms of Asia were remarkably numerous. Rapin was here in French, though very rare in that language. Mr. Jefferson said that after all it was still the best history of England, for Hume's tory principles are to him insupportable. The best mode of counteracting their effect is, he thinks, to publish an edition of Hume expunging all those reflections and reasonings whose influence is so injurious. This has been attempted by Baxter, but he has injured the work by making other material abridgements. D'Avila was there in Italian, in Mr. Jefferson's opinion, one of the most entertaining books he ever read. I was surprised to find here two little volumes on Chronology by Count Potocki of St. Petersburg. Mr. Jefferson has also a fine collection of Saxon and Moeso Gothic books, among them Alfred's translations of Orosius and Boethius, and shewed us some attempts he had made at facilitating the study of this language. He thought the singularity of the letters one of the greatest difficulties and proposed publishing the Saxon books in four columns, the first to contain the Saxon, the second the same in Roman characters, the third a strictly verbal translation and the fourth a free one. Mr. Jefferson said the French dictionary of Trévoux was better than that of the Academy, thought Charron's "de la Sagesse" an excellent work and brought us a commentary and review of Montesquieu published by Duane the translator from the French manuscript, which he called the best book on politics which had been published for a century and agreed with its author in his opinion of Montesquieu.

Of all branches of learning, however, that relating to the history of North and South America is the most perfectly displayed in this library. The collection on this subject is without a question the most valuable in the world. Here are the works of all the Spanish travellers in America and the great work of De Brie in which he has collected latin translations of the smaller works published by the earliest visitors of America whose original publications are now lost. It is finely printed and adorned with many plates. Here also is a copy of the letters of Fernando Cortes in Spanish, one of a small edition, and the copy retained by the Editor the Cardinal Archbishop of Toledo for himself, but given by him to the American Consul for Mr. Jefferson. This work contains the official letters of Cortes to his court, his maps of the country and plates representing the dresses, armour and other contents of the treasury of the Mexican Sovereigns. We saw here also some beautiful modern manuscripts, one of a work which had been suppressed in France, most of the Greek Romances.

Mr. Jefferson took us from his library into his bed chamber where, on a table before the fire, stood a polygraph with which he said he always wrote.

Mr. Jefferson took his accustomed ride before dinner and on his return told us that the ice was crowded and thick on the banks of the Rivanna and had carried away thirty feet of his mill-dam. This was all he said on the subject and from his manner I supposed his loss was probably about one or two hundred dollars, but on our ride back to Richmond we heard it everywhere spoken of as a serious loss and the countrymen, some of them, even estimated it at $30,000. This to be sure must have been a most wonderful miscalculation, but no doubt the loss was serious.

Francis Calley Gray, *Thomas Jefferson in 1814, Being an Account of a Visit to Monticello, Virginia,* ed. Henry S. Rowe and T. Jefferson Coolidge, Jr. (Boston, 1924), 63–74. Reprinted by permission of The Club of Odd Volumes, Boston.

1. Presumably the dining room; see Ticknor's account, which follows.

⊰ 1815 ⊱

⟨

"Old Books and Young Society"

GEORGE TICKNOR —a year younger than Gray—was a native of Boston and a graduate of Dartmouth College. Although he, like Gray, had just finished his law studies, Ticknor had already resolved on going to Europe in pursuit of a scholarly career. While studying in Europe he sought out books for Jefferson; when he returned in 1819 he became the professor of modern languages at Harvard and sometimes corresponded with Jefferson on literary and educational topics. Ticknor's account continues Gray's into the third and fourth days of their visit. He wrote it as a letter to his father upon their departure. It was published in *The Life and Letters of George Ticknor* in 1876.

WE LEFT CHARLOTTESVILLE on Saturday morning, the 4th of February, for Mr. Jefferson's. He lives, you know, on a mountain, which he has named Monticello, and which, perhaps you do not know, is a synonyme for Carter's Mountain. The ascent of this steep, savage hill, was as pensive and slow as Satan's ascent to Paradise. We were obliged to wind two thirds round its sides before we reached the artificial lawn on which the house stands; and, when we had arrived there, we were about six hundred feet, I understand, above the stream which flows at its foot. It is an abrupt mountain. The fine growth of ancient forest-trees conceals its side and shades part of its summit. The prospect is admirable. . . . The lawn on the top, as I hinted, was artificially formed by cutting down the peak of the height. In its centre, and facing the southeast, Mr. Jefferson has placed his house, which is of

61

brick, two stories high in the wings, with a piazza in front of a receding centre. It is built, I suppose, in the French style. You enter, by a glass folding-door, into a hall which reminds you of Fielding's "Man of the Mountain," [1] by the strange furniture of its walls. On one side hang the head and horns of an elk, a deer, and a buffalo; another is covered with curiosities which Lewis and Clarke found in their wild and perilous expedition. On the third, among many other striking matters, was the head of a mammoth, or, as Cuvier calls it, a mastodon, containing the only *os frontis,* Mr. Jefferson tells me, that has yet been found. On the fourth side, in odd union with a fine painting of the Repentance of Saint Peter, is an Indian map on leather, of the southern waters of the Missouri, and an Indian representation of a bloody battle, handed down in their traditions.

Through this hall—or rather museum—we passed to the dining room, and sent our letters to Mr. Jefferson, who was of course in his study. Here again we found ourselves surrounded with paintings that seemed good.

We had hardly time to glance at the pictures before Mr. Jefferson entered; and if I was astonished to find Mr. Madison short and somewhat awkward, I was double astonished to find Mr. Jefferson, whom I had always supposed to be a small man, more than six feet high, with dignity in his appearance, and ease and graciousness in his manners. . . . He rang, and sent to Charlottesville for our baggage, and, as dinner approached, took us to the drawing-room,—a large and rather elegant room, twenty or thirty feet high,—which, with the hall I have described, composed the whole centre of the house, from top to bottom. The floor of this room is tessellated. It is formed of alternate diamonds of cherry and beech, and kept polished as highly as if it were of fine mahogany.

Here are the best pictures of the collection. Over the fireplace is the Laughing and Weeping Philosophers, dividing the world between them; on its right, the earliest navigators to America,—Columbus, Americus Vespuccius, Magellan, etc.,—copied, Mr. Jefferson said, from originals in the Florence Gallery. Farther round, Mr. Madison in the plain, Quaker-like dress of his youth, Lafayette in his Revolutionary uniform, and Franklin in the dress in which we always see him. There were other pictures, and a copy of Raphael's Transfiguration.

We conversed on various subjects until dinner-time, and at dinner were introduced to the grown members of his family. These are his only remaining child, Mrs. Randolph, her husband, Colonel Randolph, and the two oldest of their unmarried children, Thomas Jefferson and Ellen; and I assure you I have seldom met a pleasanter party.

The evening passed away pleasantly in general conversation, of which Mr. Jefferson was necessarily the leader. I shall probably surprise you by saying that, in conversation, he reminded me of Dr. Freeman.[2] He has the same discursive manner and love of paradox, with the same appearance of sobriety and cool reason. He seems equally fond of American antiquities, and especially the antiquities of his native State, and talks of them with freedom and, I suppose, accuracy. He has, too, the appearance of that fairness and simplicity which Dr. Freeman has; and, if the parallel holds no further here, they will again meet on the ground of their love of old books and young society.

On Sunday morning, after breakfast, Mr. Jefferson asked me into his library, and there I spent the forenoon of that day as I had that of yesterday. This collection of books, now so much talked about, consists of about seven thousand volumes, contained in a suite of fine rooms, and is arranged in the catalogue, and on the shelves, according to the divisions and subdivisions of human learning by Lord Bacon. In so short a time I could not, of course, estimate its value, even if I had been competent to do so.

Perhaps the most curious single specimen—or, at least, the most characteristic of the man and expressive of his hatred of royalty—was a collection which he had bound up in six volumes, and lettered "The Book of Kings," consisting of the "Memoires de la Princesse de Bareith," two volumes; "Les Memoires de la Comtesse de la Motte," two volumes; the "Trial of the Duke of York," one volume; and *"The Book"* one volume. These documents of regal scandal seemed to be favorites with the philosopher, who pointed them out to me with a satisfaction somewhat inconsistent with the measured gravity he claims in relation to such subjects generally.

On Monday morning I spent a couple of hours with him in his study. He gave me there an account of the manner in which he passed the portion of his time in Europe which he could rescue from public business; told me that while he was in France he had formed a plan of going to Italy, Sicily, and Greece, and that he should have executed it, if he had not left Europe in the full conviction that he should immediately return there, and find a better opportunity. He spoke of my intention to go, and, without my even hinting any purpose to ask him for letters, told me that he was now seventy-two years old, and that most of his friends and correspondents in Europe had died in the course of the twenty-seven years since he left France, but that he would gladly furnish me with the means of becoming acquainted with some of the remainder, if I would give him a month's notice, and regretted that their number was so reduced.

The afternoon and evening passed as on the two days previous; for everything is done with such regularity, that when you know how one day is filled, I suppose you know how it is with the others. At eight o'clock the first bell is rung in the great hall, and at nine the second summons you to the breakfast-room, where you find everything ready. After breakfast every one goes, as inclination leads him, to his chamber, the drawing-room, or the library. The children retire to their school-room with their mother, Mr. Jefferson rides to his mills on the Rivanna, and returns at about twelve. At half past three the great bell rings, and those who are disposed resort to the drawing-room, and the rest go the dining-room at the second call of the bell, which is at four o'clock. The dinner was always choice, and served in the French style; but no wine was set on the table till the cloth was removed. The ladies sat until about six, then retired, but returned with the tea-tray a little before seven, and spent the evening with the gentlemen; which was always pleasant, for they are obviously accustomed to join in the conversation, however high the topic may be. At about half past ten, which seemed to be their usual hour of retiring, I went to my chamber, found there a fire, candle, and a servant in waiting to receive my orders for the morning, and in the morning was waked by his return to build the fire.

To-day, Tuesday, we told Mr. Jefferson that we should leave Monticello in the afternoon. He seemed much surprised, and said as much as politeness would permit on the badness of the roads and the prospect of bad weather, to induce us to remain longer. It was evident, I thought, that they had calculated on our staying a week. At dinner, Mr. Jefferson again urged us to stay, not in an oppressive way, but with kind politeness; and when the horses were at the door, asked if he should not send them away; but, as he found us resolved on going, he bade us farewell in the heartiest style of Southern hospitality, after thrice reminding me that I must write to him for letters to his friends in Europe. I came away almost regretting that the coach returned so soon, and thinking, with General Hamilton, that he was a perfect gentleman in his own house.

Two little incidents which occurred while we were at Monticello should not be passed by. The night before we left, young Randolph came up late from Charlottesville, and brought the astounding news that the English had been defeated before New Orleans by General Jackson. Mr. Jefferson had made up his mind that the city would fall, and told me that the English would hold it permanently—or for some time—by a force of Sepoys from the East Indies. He had gone to bed, like the rest of us; but of course his grandson went to his chamber with the paper containing the news. But the old philosopher refused to open his door, saying he could wait till the morning; and when we met at breakfast I found he had not yet seen it.

One morning, when he came back from his ride, he told Mr. Randolph, very quietly, that the dam had been carried away the night before. From his manner, I supposed it an affair of small consequence, but at Charlottesville, on my way to Richmond, I found the country ringing with it. Mr. Jefferson's great dam was gone, and it would cost $30,000 to rebuild it.

There is a breathing of notional philosophy in Mr. Jefferson,—in his dress, his house, his conversation. His setness, for instance, in wearing very sharp toed shoes, corduroy small-clothes, and red plush waistcoast, which have been laughed at till he might perhaps wisely have dismissed them.

So, though he told me he thought Charron, "De la Sagesse," the best treatise on moral philosophy ever written, and an obscure Review of Montesquieu, by Dupont de Nemours,[3] the best political work that had been printed for fifty years,—though he talked very freely of the natural impossibility that one generation should bind another to pay a public debt, and of the expediency of vesting all the legislative authority of a State in one branch, and the executive authority in another, and leaving them to govern it by joint discretion,—I considered such opinions simply as curious *indicia* of an extraordinary character.

Life, Letters, and Journals of George Ticknor (Boston, 1909), 1:34–38.

1. "The Man of the Hill" in Henry Fielding, *Tom Jones,* bk. VIII, chs. 10–15.

2. The Reverend James Freeman, first Unitarian minister of King's Chapel, Boston.

3. In fact, Destutt de Tracy.

ᴀᴄ 1816 ᴾᴸ

𝒥

An Expatriate Frenchman
Eyes the Museum

THE BARON DE MONTLEZUN, an elderly Frenchman unhappy with the new regime at home, was on his second tour of the United States in 1816 when he visited Monticello as well as Madison's Montpelier and James Monroe's Highlands. Loosely written, his account is especially interesting for its detailed information on Jefferson's "museum" It was edited and published in an English translation in 1943.

Friday, September 20, 181[6].
Trip from Montpelier to Monticello (Albemarle)
AT SEVEN O'CLOCK IN THE MORNING. I left Bentivoglio, Couper's Tavern; and again traversing the woods at a distance of three miles I passed in front of Judge Gordon's house, whence I forded the North [Rivanna] River near Milton, a very small village.

Monticello is located three miles further, on a considerable height, whence one overlooks the horizons for a distance of forty-five miles. I arrived at two o'clock, just when ex-president Jefferson was sitting down to dinner; he had to leave immediately afterwards to visit a piece of land he owns near New London,[1] in Virginia.

Mr. Jefferson, after showing me the principal vantage points roundabout, and also several curious objects, invited me to dinner.

On arising from the table, and after politely pressing me to stay at his house in spite of his leaving, he got into a four-horse barouche, accompanied by Mrs. Randolph and two of his grand-daughters.

I went back into the house with Mr. Randolph junior, who showed me the museum, situated in the entrance of the house. Extremely rare things are seen in it, some of which could not be found anywhere else, among others the upper jaw of a mammoth. It was found in Kentucky. It was from it that Mr. Peale made the model with which he completed his mammoth in the Philadelphia museum. The head is complete, but the lower jaw does not belong to the same specimen. Two other very curious objects are: (1) An Indian picture representing a battle; it is on buffalo hide, about five feet square. There are four lines of warriors. On each line there are horses painted red and green opposite each other, as are the warriors, armed and dressed in the manner of the savages. (2) A map, also on buffalo hide, six feet square. without the least defect. It represents a part of the course of the Missouri, and is easily understood although crudely traced. The explanations were written in French by interpreters.

There is also a mammoth's tusk and an elephant's, with a tooth of the latter to show how much it differs from those of the mammoth; the latter being conical and indicating a carnivore, while the other, flat and streaked at the crown, a fructivore.

A head of a gigantic ram; it is supposed that the animal of which it was a part belongs to the primitive race which used to exist in North America.

Mr. Randolph then showed me the pictures and portraits which adorn the different rooms.

The portraits of Washington, La Fayette, Adams, Franklin, Walter Raleigh, Amerigo Vespucci, Columbus, Bacon, Locke, Newton, etc., etc.

Pictures: a dead man arising from the tomb to testify; the surrender of Cornwallis in October, 1781, at Yorktown, in Virginia; Diogenes looking for a man; Democritus and Heraclitus, etc., etc., etc.

I also saw: a bear's claw, from the Missouri. This species is larger and much more ferocious than the others; a mammoth's tusk; several teeth of the same animal; the thigh-bone of the same.

The mammoth's head seen here is formed, as I have already said, of the upper jaw, which is perfect, and two halves of the lower jaw coming from different specimens; one of the halves is larger than the other.

A European coat of mail which those who fought with the Indians used in the early wars. By this means they were without danger of being wounded by the arrows.

Antlers of the American elk, and of other animals of the same type.

The antlers of the elk are quite large; these animals, as well as the buffalo and several others, have been destroyed in the parts of Virginia where the population has become dense. They are found in the territory of the Ohio where the great numbers of hunters have forced them to take refuge.

Two stone busts, sculptured by the Indians, one representing a man and the other a woman. The faces are hideous and very crudely executed. They were doubtless designated for worship, and have much similarity with those divinities of the Egyptians and Orientals whose pictures are seen engraved in most of the books which treat of those people.

A little Indian hatchet in a kind of polished porphyry; the upper part is in the form of a pipe; a figure of an animal, in the same kind of stone; various petrifactions; bows, arrows, spears and a host of objects made by the Indians; a life-size marble statue, similar to that of Cleopatra. She is lying down; a serpent is twined around her left arm. Copy from the antique. Mr. Jefferson thinks that it represents Ariadne.

Elephant's tooth. This tooth, which indicates an herbivorous animal, is entirely different from those of the mammoth. Nevertheless it is generally believed that the latter is nothing other than an elephant. . . .

The house is an irregular octagon, with portals at the east and west, and peristyles at the north and south. Its extent, including peristyles and portals, is about one hundred and ten feet by ninety. The exterior, in Doric style, is surmounted by balustrades. The interior of the house is decorated in the different styles of architecture, with the exception of the composite. The vestibule is Ionic; the dining room Doric, the drawing room Corinthian and the dome Attic. The rooms are decorated with various forms of these styles, in their true proportions, after Palladio. There are eleven rooms on the ground floor, six on the second story and four in the attic. From north to south, on the same level as the cellars, there is a passage-way of three hundred feet, leading to two wings or rows of one-story buildings, equidistant from the ends of the house, each row terminating in a two-story pavilion. The top [of the passage-way] forms a gallery and is adorned with a balustrade à la chinoise which is not very high in order not to interfere with the view. To the south are the kitchens, servants' quarters and other appurtenances. To the north, the ice-house, coach-houses, etc. The library contains rare works in the principal languages.

Mr. Jefferson owns a large collection of mathematical and optical instruments, and several Indian curios. Among the latter are two busts of a man and a woman, seated Indian fashion; they were found buried in the State of Tennessee; they are of stone and much damaged. In the vestibule one also observed a picture of a battle between the Pawnee and the Osages, as well as a map of the course of the Missouri on tanned buffalo hide. One also sees bows, arrows, poisoned spears, peace pipes, mocassins, etc., with various articles of clothing and kitchen utensils of the Mandans and other nations of the Missouri.

The same place contains also the colossal bust of Mr. Jefferson by [Ceracchi]. It is supported on a broken column, the pedestal of which has for ornament the representation of the twelve tribes of Israel and the twelve signs of the zodiac.

A statue of Cleopatra, reclining and supine to the stings of the asp.

The busts of Voltaire and Turgot, in plaster, as well as the model of the Great Pyramid of Egypt.

In the drawing room the bust of Emperor Alexander, that of the usurper Bonaparte, and Venus sleeping.

Around the dining room are the busts of General Washington, Doctor Franklin, the Marquis de Lafayette, and Paul Jones.

The collection of pictures is precious: among others one sees the Ascension by Poussin, the Holy Family by Raphael, the Flagellation of Christ by Rubens, the Crucifixion by Guido Reni, along with several other subjects drawn from the Bible and history, executed by the outstanding masters, and a large number of prints, medals, medallions, etc., of distinguished people and famous events.

The natural history curios are very numerous: they consist of mammoth bones, horns, antlers or tusks of various animals, a head of a mountain goat, petrifications, crystallisations, minerals, shells, etc.

The lands tributary to Monticello, it is said, form a total of eleven thousand acres, of which about fifteen hundred are under cultivation. In addition, Mr. Jefferson possesses in Bedford County a property from which he gets annually forty thousand pounds of tobacco and all the grain necessary for the consumption and upkeep of his numerous farms. There are also merino sheep, broad-tailed rams from the Cape, etc. Monticello has a wool and a cotton manufactory, and a nail shop. . . .

Mr. Jefferson is seventy-three years old and doesn't appear to be more than sixty-three. His grandson, who is six feet four inches tall, told me that he was of average size among the inhabitants of the surrounding mountains. The women whom I chanced to see around here are pretty, sprightly and tall.

Mr. Randolph showed me a personal map, indicating the trip of Captains Lewis and Clark, who, followed by forty-four men, crossed that whole vast territory which stretches from the Atlantic to the Southern Sea. . . .

At four o'clock, I took leave of Mr. Randolph to go to Mr. Monroe's, three miles from ex-president Jefferson's home.

I arrived there at six; and the colonel, Secretary of State, greeted me most civilly.

[Baron de Montlezun], "A Frenchman Visits Albemarle, 1816," tr. and ed. J. M. Carrier and L. G. Moffatt *Papers of the Albemarle County Historical Society* 4 (1943–44): 45–52. Reprinted by permission.

1. Poplar Forest, in Bedford County, about eighty miles south of Monticello.

⚔ 1816 ⚔

⅃

"Call It Olympus"

THE SON OF JEFFERSON'S FRIEND the famous physician Benjamin Rush, Richard Rush was among the most promising of the second generation of American statesmen. In 1816, when he made his pilgrimage to Monticello, he was attorney general of the United States. His eloquent response to this Olympus, where the fog never ascended, is contained in a letter to Charles Jared Ingersoll at home in Philadelphia.

MONTICELLO IS A CURIOSITY! Artificial to a high degree; in many respects superb. If it had not been called Monticello, I would call it Olympus, and Jove its occupant. In genius, in elevation, in the habits and enjoyments of his life, he [Jefferson] is wonderfully lifted above most mortals. The fog I was told never rises to the level of his mountain; and it is just so with what the newspapers say of him. Further, the dew does not fall on it; nor are there any *insects* there; nor, by consequence, any *birds!* Now figure to yourself a house exalted upon such an eminence as all this bespeaks, and that house, thus as it were in the sky, decked off with art and wealth, and you have Monticello. I saw nothing so cheap as a print on the walls; nothing but paintings or statuary, with curious assemblages of artificial or natural objects forming quite a museum.

He lamented the loss of his library, and expects an importation of books this fall from Europe. His chief reading is the ancient classics, in the originals. He admitted that they were of no use, but he exclaimed, "they are such a luxury." He reads, he says, no longer for knowledge, but for gratification. I need not tell you with what open doors he lives, as you well know his mountain is made a sort of Mecca.

Richard Rush to Charles Jared Ingersoll, Oct. 9, 1816, *The Letters and Papers of Richard Rush,* ed. Anthony M. Brescia, microfilm edition (Wilmington, Del., 1980).

⤚ 1817 ⤙

A Friendly Englishman at Monticello

LIEUTENANT FRANCIS HALL of the British army, touring the eastern United States in 1816–17, came to Monticello by way of the Shenandoah Valley after observing the session of Congress in Washington. Unlike most educated Englishmen of the time, he admired Jefferson and republican institutions. Only an overnight guest, Hall supplemented his account of Jefferson's conversation with opinions recently aired in the press. Published in London in 1818, Hall's *Travels* was immediately republished in Boston.

HAVING AN INTRODUCTION TO MONTICELLO, I ascended his little mountain on a fine morning, which gave the situation its due effect. The whole of the sides and base are covered with forest, through which roads have been cut circularly, so that the winding may be shortened or prolonged at pleasure: the summit is an open lawn, near to the south side of which the house is built, with its garden just descending the brow: the saloon, or central hall, is ornamented with several pieces of antique sculpture, Indian arms, Mammoth bones, and other curiosities collected from various parts of the Union. I found Mr. Jefferson tall in person, but stooping and lean with old age, thus exhibiting that fortunate mode of bodily decay, which strips the frame of its most cumbersome parts, leaving it still strength of muscle and activity of limb. His deportment was exactly such as the Marquis de Chastellux describes it, above thirty years ago: "At first serious, nay even cold," but in a very short time relaxing into a most agreeable amenity; with an unabated flow of conversation on the most interesting topicks, discussed in the most gentlemanly and philosophical manner. I walked with him round his grounds, to visit his pet trees, and improvements of various kinds: during the walk, he pointed out to my observation a conical mountain, rising singly at the edge of the southern horizon of the landscape: its distance he said, was 40 miles, and its dimensions those of the greater Egyptian pyramid; so that it accurately represents the appearance of the pyramid at the same distance; there is small cleft visible on its summit, through which, the true meridian of Monticello exactly passes: its most singular property, however, is, that on different occasions it looms, or alters its appearance, becoming sometimes cylindrical, sometimes square, and sometimes assuming the form of an inverted cone. Mr. Jefferson had not been able to connect this phenomenon with any particular season, or state of the atmosphere, except, that it most commonly occurred in the forenoon. He observed, that it was not only wholly unaccounted for by the laws of vision, but that it had not as yet engaged the attention of philosophers so far as to acquire a name; that of looming, being in fact, a term applied by sailors, to appearances of a similar kind at sea. The Blue Mountains are also observed to loom, though not in so remarkable a degree.

It must be interesting to recall and preserve the political sentiments of a man who has held so distinguished a station in publick life as Mr. Jefferson. He seemed to consider much of the freedom and happiness of America to arise from local circumstances. "Our population," he observed, "has an elasticity, by which it would fly off from oppressive taxation." He instanced the beneficial effects of a free government, in the case of New Orleans, where many proprietors who were in a state of indigence under the dominion of Spain, have risen to sudden wealth, solely by the rise in the value of land, which followed a change of government. Their ingenuity in mechanical inventions, agricultural improvements, and that mass of general information to be found among Americans of all ranks and conditions, he ascribed to that ease of circumstances, which afforded them leisure to cultivate their minds, after the cultivation of their lands was completed. In fact, I have frequently been surprised to find mathematical and other useful works in houses, which seemed to have little pretension to the luxury of learning. Another cause, Mr. Jefferson observed, might be discovered in the many court and county meetings, which brought men frequently together on publick business, and thus gave them habits, both of thinking and of expressing their thoughts on subjects, which in other countries are confined to the consideration of the privileged few. Mr. Jefferson has not the reputation of being very friendly to England: we should, however, be aware, that a partiality in this respect is not absolutely the duty of an American citizen; neither is it to be expected that the policy of our government should be regarded in foreign countries, with the same complacency with which it is looked upon by ourselves: but whatever may be his sentiments in this respect, politeness naturally repressed any offensive expression of them: he talked of our affairs with candour, and apparent good will, though leaning, perhaps, to the gloomier side of the picture. He did not perceive by what means we could be extricated from our present financial embarrassments, without some kind of revolution in our government: on my replying, that our habits were remarkably steady, and that great sacrifices would be made to prevent a violent catastrophe, he acceded to the observation, but demanded, if those who made the sacrifices, would not require some political reformation in return. His repugnance was strongly marked to the depotic principles of Bonaparte, and he seemed to consider France under Louis XVI as scarcely capable of a republican form of government; but added, that the present generation of Frenchmen had grown up with sounder notions, which would probably lead to their emancipation. Relative to the light in which he views the conduct of the Allied Sovereigns, I cannot do better than insert a letter of his to Dr. Logan, dated 18th October, 1815, and published in the American Newspapers:

> *Dear Sir,—I thank you for the extract in yours of August 16th, respecting the Emperour Alexander. It arrived here a day or two after I had left this place, from which I have been absent about seven or eight weeks. I had from other information, formed the most favourable opinion of the virtues of the Emperour Alexander, and considered his partiality to this country as a prominent proof of them. The magnanimity of his conduct on the first capture of Paris, still magnified every thing we had believed of him; but how he will come out of his present trial, remains to be seen: that the sufferings which France had inflicted on other countries, justified some repri-*

sals, cannot be questioned, but I have not yet learned what crimes Poland, Saxony, Belgium, Venice, Lombardy, and Genoa, had merited for them, not merely a temporary punishment, but that of permanent subjugation, and a destitution of independence and self-government. The fable of Aesop and the Lion dividing the spoils, is, I fear, becoming true history, and the moral code of Napoleon and the English government, a substitute for that of Grotius, of Puffendorf, and even of the pure doctrines of the great author of our own religion. We were safe ourselves from Bonaparte, because he had not the British fleets at his command. We were safe from the British fleets, because they had Bonaparte at their back, but the British fleets, and the conquerors of Bonaparte, being now combined, and the Hartford nation[1] drawn off to them, we have uncommon reasons to look to our own affairs. This, however, I leave to others, offering prayers to Heaven, the only contribution of old age, for the safety of our country. Be so good as to present me affectionately to Mrs. Logan, and to accept, yourself, the assurance of my esteem and respect.

T. Jefferson.

The same anxiety for his country's independence seems to have led him to a change of opinion on the relative importance of manufactories in America. He thus expresses himself, in answer to an address from the American society for the encouragment of manufactories: "I have read with great satisfaction, the eloquent pamphlet you were so kind as to send me, and sympathize with every line of it. I was once a doubter, whether the labour of the cultivator, aided by the creative powers of the earth itself, would not produce more value than that of the manufacturer alone, and unassisted by the dead subject on which he acted; in other words, whether the more we could bring into action of the energies of our boundless territory, in addition to the labour of our citizens, the more would not be our gain. But the inventions of the latter times, by labour-saving machines, do as much now for the manufacturer, as the earth for the cultivator. Experience too, has proved that mine was but half the question; the other half is, whether dollars and cents are to be weighed in the scale against real independence. The question is then solved, at least so far as respects our own wants.

I much fear the effect on our infant establishment, of the policy avowed by Mr. Brougham, and quoted in the pamphlet. Individual British merchants may lose by the late immense importations; but British commerce and manufactories in the mass will gain, by beating down the competition of ours in our own markets, &c."

The conversation turning on American history, Mr. Jefferson related an anecdote of the Abbé Raynal, which serves to shew how history, even when it calls itself philosophical, is written. The Abbé was in company with Dr. Franklin, and several Americans at Paris, when mention chanced to be made of his anecdote of Polly Baker, related in his sixth volume,[2] upon which one of the company observed, that no such law as that alluded to in the story, existed in New England: the Abbé stoutly maintained the authenticity of his tale, when Dr. Franklin, who had hitherto remained silent, said, "I can account for all this; you took the anecdote from a newspaper of which I was at that time editor, and, happening to be very short of news, I composed and inserted the whole story." "Ah! Doctor," said the Abbé making a true French retreat, "I had rather have your stories, then other men's truths."

Mr. Jefferson preferred Botta's Italian History of the American Revolution, to any that had yet appeared, remarking, however, the inaccuracy of the speeches. Indeed, the true history of that period seems to be generally considered as lost: A remarkable letter on this point, lately appeared in print, from the venerable Mr. John Adams, to a Mr. Niles, who had solicited his aid to collect and publish a body of revolutionary speeches. He says, "Of all the speeches made in Congress, from 1774 to 1777, inclusive, of both years, not one sentence remains, except a few periods of Dr. Witherspoon, printed in his works." His concluding sentence is very strong. "In plain English, and in a few words, Mr. Niles, I consider the true history of the American revolution, and the establishment of our present constitutions, as lost for ever; and nothing but misrepresentations, or partial accounts of it, will ever be recovered."

I slept a night at Monticello, and left it in the morning, with such a feeling as the traveller quits the mouldering remains of a Grecian temple, or the pilgrim a fountain in the desert. I would indeed argue great torpor, both of understanding and heart, to have looked without veneration and interest, on the man who drew up the declaration of

American Independence; who shared in the councils by which her freedom was established; whom the unbought voice of his fellow-citizens called to the exercise of a dignity, from which his own moderation impelled him, when such example was most salutary, to withdraw; and who, while he dedicates the evening of his glorious days to the pursuits of science and literature, shuns none of the humbler duties of private life; but, having filled a seat higher than that of kings, succeeds with graceful dignity to that of the good neighbour, and becomes the friendly adviser, lawyer, physician, and even gardener of his vicinity. This is the "still small voice" of philosophy, deeper and holier than the lightnings and the earthquakes which have preceded it. What monarch would venture thus to exhibit himself in the nakedness of his humanity? On what royal brow would the laurel replace the diadem? But they who are born and educated to be kings, are not expected to be philosophers. This is a just answer, though no great compliment either to the governours or the governed.

My travels had nearly terminated at the Rivannah, which flows at the foot of Monticello: in trying to ford it, my horse and waggon were carried down the stream: I escaped with my servant, and by the aid of Mr. Jefferson's domesticks, we finally succeeded in extricating my equipage from a watery grave. The road to Richmond follows the James River, and has few features to attract notice. There are no towns, and very few villages. Of the taverns, I have only to remark, that Mrs. Tisley's is a clean, comfortable house, and that Mr. Powell is a very civil landlord.

Francis Hall, *Travels in Canada and the United States in 1816 and 1817* (London, 1818), 225–31.

1. Jefferson considered the Hartford Convention of December 1814 a disunionist conspiracy of New England Federalists.

2. That is, of Raynal's *Histoire des Deux Indes.*

7
(

A Cordial Reunion
in 1820

ISAAC BRIGGS was a Maryland Quaker, well versed in such matters as agriculture, manufactures, commerce, and navigation, who had served President Jefferson as surveyor general south of the Tennessee. Going to his post in New Orleans in 1804, Briggs had, at the president's request, mapped the route for a new road to that distant quarter of the Union so greatly enlarged by the Louisiana Purchase. Aside from the amusing story of the mysterious stranger—one wonders how many visitors went unintroduced and unnoticed—Briggs's description of his visit is chiefly interesting for Jefferson's impassioned outburst against the Missouri Compromise. Briggs incorporated his report, written as a diary, in a letter to his wife and children on November 21, 1820.

11 MO. 2—FIFTH DAY OF THE WEEK. I reached Monticello about 4 o'clock afternoon. On entering the great hall I saw sitting within the door a stranger; supposing him to be a member of the family, I asked him, "Is Thomas Jefferson at home?" He answered, "I believe he is— I am a stranger, on my way to the southward, and have called on purpose to see him. I have no one to introduce me—are you acquainted with him?" I am—thou wilt not find him difficult of access, said I; for the man seemed under considerable embarrassment. I enquired if he had announced his being in waiting. He said he had, and in a few minutes the dear, venerable old man entered the hall. I instantly met him, took his offered hand and with warmth of feeling said, "My friend Jefferson! how art thou?" With equal cordiality he

returned my salute; and then turning to the stranger saluted him, and asked us both to walk in and take a glass of wine with him. We followed him into the dining room, where were seated about a table his sister Marks, and three or four of his grand daughters, fine looking young women; Thomas Jefferson took his seat at the table, and placed me on his right hand and the stranger on his left; then turning to me, with a pleasant smile, he said, "Why, Mr. Briggs, you have grown young again."

In a short time the stranger took his leave, saying that he had parted from his company on purpose to make his respects at Monticello, and must join them again that evening in Charlottesville. As soon as he had departed, Thomas Jefferson said, "Mr. Briggs, who is that gentleman?" I answered, "I do not know—he is quite a stranger to me." "I thought he came with you." "No, I found him in the hall, when I first arrived."

I told Thomas Jefferson I proposed to spend the next day with him and the following to pursue my journey to Richmond, and that I wished to see the University of Virginia. He replied with quickness, "You must see it. I had intended to go there, the day after tomorrow, but it will be as well for me to go tomorrow, and you must ride with me."

In the course of the evening I communicated to him the remembrance of my wife and of my daughter Mary; he seemed highly gratified, and in a affectionate manner enquired after the health of my family, particularly of Mary. I delivered to him Thomas Moore's message—"his Respects"—and that he had continually regretted, since it happened, that he did not visit him, when, in the course of his duties as Engineer in 1818, he had passed within one mile of Monticello. "I blamed Mr. Moore," said he. "Where is he now?" At home in Maryland. "Is he well?" He is well. About 8 o'clock, after a very friendly, social and agreeable evening so far, he rose from his seat and said to me, "I feel that I am an old man, and it is proper for me to retire early to bed, you will excuse me and choose your own time." I remained with his daughter and her daughters, the wife and daughters of Thomas M. Randolph, Governor of Virginia, till about 10 o'clock, when I retired for the night.

11 mo. 3—sixth day of the week. This morning after breakfast, Thomas Jefferson and I rode to see the University of Virginia. It is

Monticello, first version. Accepted elevation, 1771.

ourtesy of the Massachusetts Historical Society.)

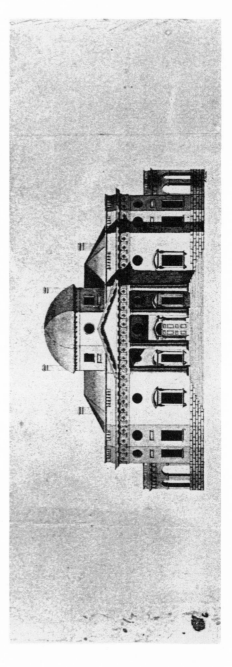

Monticello: west front and plan of first floor and dependencies.
Drawing by Robert Mills, about 1803. (*Courtesy of the Massachusetts Historical Society.*)

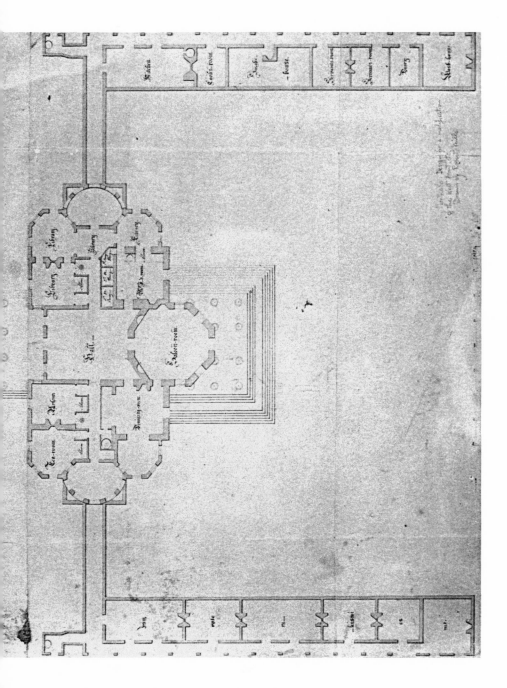

West front and lawn with children. Watercolor by Jane Bradick, about 182

Monticello afte
Engraving after a painting by Georg

efferson's death.
Cooke. (From *Family Magazine*, 1837.)

situated about 4 miles from Monticello. The operations of tuition have not yet commenced, nor are the buildings finished, but the work is in active progress, and so far advanced, as to exhibit, to one acquainted with these things, a very good idea of the design, scope and probable fruits of the institution. It consists of three rows of buildings,[1] each row a thousand feet long and having two fronts. The plan of it was furnished by Thomas Jefferson—it is going on under his special superintendence and direction—it occupies a great portion of his time, his personal attendance is frequent and unremitted—it seems to be his favorite employment and the solace of his declining years. His 77th year finds him strong, active, and in full possession of a sound mind. He rides a *trotting* horse and sits on him as straight as a young man. Compared with him, Madison, although ten years younger, looks like a little old man. Returning to Monticello from the University of Virginia (which promises to be the greatest and most extensive establishment of the kind in the United States) we had much conversation. Among other political points, that which has been called the Missouri question stood prominent. He said that nothing had happened since the revolution, which gave him so much anxiety and so many disquieting fears for the safety and happiness of his country. "I fear," said he, "that much mischief has been done already, but if they carry matters to extremities again at the approaching session of Congress, nothing short of Almighty power can save us. The Union will be broken. All the horrors of civil war, embittered by local jealousies and mutual recriminations, will ensue. Bloodshed, rapine and cruelty will soon roam at large, will desolate our once happy land and turn the fruitful field into a howling wilderness. Out of such a state of things will naturally grow a war of extermination toward the African in our land. Instead of improving the condition of this poor, afflicted, degraded race, terminating, in the ordering of wisdom, in equal liberty and the enjoyment of equal rights (in which direction public opinion is advancing with rapid strides) the course pursued, by those who make high professions of humanity and of friendship for them, would involve them as well as us in certain destruction. I believe there are many, very many, who are *quite honest* in their humane views and feelings toward this people, lending their efforts, with amiable but misguided zeal, to those leaders—those master spirits, who raise the whirlwind and direct the storm—who are *not honest,* who wear humanity as a mask, whose aim is power, and who 'would wade through slaughter to a throne and shut the gates of mercy on mankind.'² I have considered the United States as owing to the world an example, and that this is their solemn duty—a steady, peaceful example of morality and happiness in society at large, of moderation and wisdom in government, and of civil and religious liberty—an example, which, by its mild and steady light, would be far more powerful than the sword in correcting abuses—in teaching mankind that they can, if they will, govern themselves, and of relieving them from the oppressions of kingcraft and priestcraft. But if our Union be broken, this duty will be sacrificed—this bright example will be lost—it will be worse than lost. The predictions of our enemies will be fulfilled, in the estimation of the world, that we were not wise enough for self government. It would be said that the fullest and fairest experiment had been made—and had *failed;* and the chains of despotism would be rivetted more firmly than ever." This is the substance; I do not pretend to recollect, *exactly,* although I believe very *nearly,* his words, for his manner was impressive. I told him my anxiety had been very great, on the same subject, and very much in the same way.

On another point, he enquired, "Mr. Briggs, did Congress ever allow you compensation for exploring and locating a Post road from Washington to New Orleans?"—No; the utmost they could be brought to do was to balance my accounts. "Did they not avail the public of your labors—did they not use the road?"—O yes, they adopted the road, and it is still used, nearly as I reported it. "Well, I think, the refusal to compensate you for that service is one of the most disgraceful things Congress have ever done."

After our return to Monticello, he left me in the hall, or drawing room, for a few minutes, and went into another room. Coming to me again, with something in his hand, he said, "Will your daughter, Mary, accept of this as a memorial of me?" I replied, "She will most thankfully. Thou hast not, in the world, a more enthusiastic admirer than she is."

A company of visitors, male and female, collected in the drawing room, before dinner. My friend Jefferson introduced me to each one, in the manner following, "Mr. Briggs, the Engineer, who is to shew us how to navigate across the mountains."

After dinner the company departed, and I spent the afternoon and evening in the delightful society of Thomas Jefferson, his sister [Anna] Marks, his daughter Martha Randolph, her daughters Ellen, Cornelia, Virginia, Mary, and Septimia, and Browse Trist, the son of a former acquaintance of mine in New Orleans. Thomas Jefferson, as usual, retired about 8; and I continued until 10, chatting with Martha Randolph and her highly polished and highly instructed daughters. It seems to be a matter of equal facility with them to write or converse, in French, Spanish, Italian, or their mother tongue.

11 mo. 4—seventh day of the week. After breakfast, I asked for my horse, and for a description of the road to Richmond. Thomas Jefferson rose to take leave of me, and, in a manner which left no doubt of sincerity, said, "I am sorry you cannot stay with us another day." I had like to have forgotten to mention, that, in conversation last evening, Thomas Jefferson, recounting over past events, dwelt with apparent satisfaction on his intimate acquaintance with Thomas Pleasants of Goochland. This was uncle Thomas Pleasants, cousin Deborah Stabler's father. About 9 o'clock, I departed from Monticello; after sunset, I arrived at Hayden's 35 miles; and the next evening (11 mo. 5—first day) in Richmond 45 miles more. From Monticello to Richmond, 80 miles.

Isaac Briggs to Hannah Briggs and Children, Nov. 21, 1820, Isaac Briggs Notebook (acc. no. 38–530), Manuscripts Division, Special Collections Department, University of Virginia Library.

1. An error (there are four rows) probably arising from the early state of the building in 1820.

2. Thomas Gray, *Elegy in a Country Churchyard,* stanza 17.

$\backsim\!\!\prec$ 1 8 2 4 $\succ\!\!\sim$

γ

A Book Peddler
at Monticello

SAMUEL WHITCOMB, JR., was a well-traveled Yankee book peddler, thirty-two years of age, when he ascended Jefferson's mountain in 1824 in quest of a sale but, failing that, was rewarded instead with fascinating conversation. His report of Jefferson's opinions on a range of subjects, including religion, is quite consistent with the evidence of Jefferson's writings; the character Whitcomb gives to the Sage of Monticello, on the other hand, is in some respects at variance with the impressions of most visitors. Whitcomb's memorandum of his "interview" was first published in 1949.

Charlottesville, Va.
Monday Morn'g, 31 May, 1824.
BETWEEN 8 & 9 o'clk. called on Mr. Jefferson. The boy conducted and left me at the door and I knocked. Mr. Jefferson came himself. I approached and shook hands with him and he asked me in. I opened by saying I had no introduction to him but a new publication for which I was getting subscribers. He replied he never subscribed to anything. I told him of my work and he said it was a very bad work.[1] Mitford misrepresents the Democrats and distorts facts, etc. etc. I turned the subject and we talked about

1st: The right of the Georgians to the Cherokee lands,
2nd: The character of the Indians,
3rd: The character of the Negroes,
4th: The Tariff,

5th: The disposition of Gt. Britain towards Spain and the United States,

6th: The Being of God,

7th: The character of Christ and His religion,

8th: The Christian clergy and Theological Controversy.

1st—He is decidedly opposed to the Georgia Claim. Says she is the most greedy of land of any State in the Union. That the Indians are under no obligation to sell these lands, that they have an original title to them.

2nd—He appears to think the Indians will all dwindle away and be lost in our race by amalgamation.

3rd—Says the south agrees with the Negroes best—that the experiment now making at Hayti is very interesting. He hopes well of their minds though has never seen evidence of genius among them, but they are possessed of the best hearts of any people in the world. Great levity of character, etc. On account of the prejudice of our Nation against the black, he would defer treating with the haytians as long as possible, but we must certainly acknowledge their independence.

4th—The Tariff would produce great excitement at the South. It was very unjust—like taking a shilling off of every dollar the southern people paid.

5th—Has full confidence in the disposition of Gt. Britain towards the freedom of South America and the United States because it is for their interest to be friendly.

6th—I asked what book was best writen on the Being of God. He could not tell me, referred to Clark.[2] I advocated materialism and atheism. He professed to believe there is a Supreme Being. Inferred it from the appearance of nature—particularly from the redeeming spirit of the Universe. The evidence of past revolutions and the recovery of the Earth from those Shocks. Said he used to read on those subjects a good deal many years ago. I observed that if the Being of God was admitted it seemed to go far toward proving the Truth of and preparing the way for the admission of Christianity. He differed from me. He thought (here he evidently had said more than he meant and endeavored to qualify it by observing) that Jesus was one of the best men who ever lived. The Theism of the Hebrews was very impure and their morality very unsocial in His day and He had tried to give them more correct view of the Deity and had taught them to be philanthropic, etc. But said I, how could He make such pretensions to Divinity and—"He never did so" interrupted Mr. J. Well said I He professed to have Divine Aid in working miracles. "No He did not— He doubtless thought He was inspired for the whole system of the Hebrews had been built on that idea." He remarked in reply to me that Paul was the first who had perverted the Doctrines of Christ. I made some remarks and concluded by saying that the Clergy in our Country were investigating these subjects with considerable independence. He dissented and expressed himself warmly in a phrase which I suppose was not English but some other language "The Clergy were all ——" It was evident that he thought little of Theological investigations. I concluded by remarking my opinion of Dr. Priestly to which he said he had read all of his works and thought very highly of him. He said something about his memory being defective. I replied that I thought he appeared very active and well for a man of his years, mentioned my aged grandparent and inadvertently asked if he was over 80; he said 81 but appeared rather gloomy and displeased.

Having been with him about an hour and feeling embarrassed at the effect my question had produced, I took my leave of him neither of us so well pleased with each other as at first.

He is tall and very straight excepting his neck which appears limber and inclined to crook. His hair is long and thin. His eyes light and weak, but somewhat severe. He is more homely, plain and uninteresting, common and undignified than I was prepared to expect. I should not take him for a generous man. He is more positive, decided and passionate than I had expected. I should think him less of a philosopher than a partizan. His manners are much the most agreeable part of him. They are artificial, he shrugs his shoulders when talking, has much of the Frenchman, is rapid, varying, volatile, eloquent, amusing. I should not think him (did I not know his age) much over 60 or 65 years.

He alluded to his being troubled with extensive correspondence but said he could read with as much ease and pleasure as ever—Can see in the day time without glasses.

When speaking of the Indians he observed that in a conversation with a chief he had told him that both his daughters married descendents of Pocahontas. This he evidently is proud of.

His house is rather old and going to decay; appearances about his yard and hill are rather slovenly. It commands an extensive prospect but it being a misty cloudy day, I could see but little of the surrounding scenery.

Mr. Jefferson is said to be careful when talking about the Presidential election but is in favor of Crawford.

Samuel Whitcomb, Jr., "An Interview with Thomas Jefferson," May 3, 1824, typescript (acc. no. 2816), Manuscripts Division, Special Collections Department, University of Virginia Library.

1. William Mitford's *History of Greece,* which Jefferson knew from its first publication and which was appearing in a new edition.

2. Samuel Clarke's *Discourse concerning the Being and Attributes of God* (1705) was a classic of Deism.

〒

A Yankee Congressman
Pens a Portrait

DANIEL WEBSTER, New Englands's rising political star, visited Monticello in company with George Ticknor and his wife in December 1824 and afterwards made a memorandum of his impressions of Jefferson and his conversation. Webster, of course, was still a Federalist, politically opposed to Jefferson and his Virginia successors. The portrait was sharply drawn; in the opinion of Jefferson's grandchildren it was inaccurate in certain details, for instance "small eyes," wrists of "extraordinary size," and "very much neglected" dress. Webster's notes on particular topics of conversation, such as Patrick Henry, are omitted here. The memorandum was first published in *Private Correspondence of Daniel Webster*, edited by Fletcher Webster, in 1857.

December, 1824.

MR. JEFFERSON is now between eighty-one and eighty-two, above six feet high, of an ample, long frame, rather thin and spare. His head, which is not peculiar in its shape, is set rather forward on his shoulders; and his neck being long, there is, when he is walking or conversing, an habitual protrusion of it. It is still well covered with hair, which having been once red, and now turning gray, is an indistinct sandy color.

His eyes are small, very light, and now neither brilliant nor striking. His chin is rather long, but not pointed. His nose small, regular in its outline, and the nostrils a little elevated. His mouth is well formed and still filled with teeth; it is strongly compressed, bearing an expression of contentment and benevolence. His complexion, formerly light and freckled, now bears the marks of age and cutaneous affection. His limbs are uncommonly long; his hands and feet very large, and his wrists of an extraordinary size. His walk is not precise and military, but easy and swinging. He stoops a little, not so much from age as from natural formation. When sitting, he appears short, partly from a rather lounging habit of sitting, and partly from the disproportionate length of his limbs.

His dress, when in the house, is a gray surtout coat, kerseymere stuff waistcoat, with an under one faced with some material of a dingy red. His pantaloons are very long and loose, and of the same color as his coat. His stockings are woolen either white or gray; and his shoes of the kind that bear his name.[1] His whole dress is very much neglected, but not slovenly. He wears a common round hat. His dress, when on horseback, is a gray straight-bodied coat and a spencer of the same material, both fastened with large pearl buttons. When we first saw him, he was riding; and, in addition to the above articles of apparel, wore round his throat a knit white woolen tippet, in the place of a cravat, and black velvet gaiters under his pantaloons. His general appearance indicates an extraordinary degree of health, vivacity, and spirit. His sight is still good, for he needs glasses only in the evening. His hearing is generally good, but a number of voices in animated conversation confuses it.

Mr. Jefferson rises in the morning as soon as he can see the hands of his clock, which is directly opposite his bed, and examines his thermometer immediately, as he keeps a regular meteorological diary. He employs himself chiefly in writing till breakfast, which is at nine. From that time, till dinner, he is in his library, excepting that in fair weather he rides on horseback from seven to fourteen miles. Dines at four, returns to the drawing-room at six, when coffee is brought in, and passes the evening till nine in conversation. His habit of retiring at that hour is so strong, that it has become essential to his health and comfort. His diet is simple, but he seems restrained only by his taste. His breakfast is tea and coffee, bread always fresh from the oven, of which he does not seem afraid, with sometimes a slight accompaniment of cold meat. He enjoys his dinner well, taking with his meat a large proportion of vegetables. He has a strong preference for the wines of the continent, of which he has many sorts of excellent quality, having been more than commonly successful in his mode of importing and preserving them. Among others, we found the following, which are very rare in this country, and apparently not at all injured by transportation: L'Ednau, Muscat, Samian, and Blanchette de Limoux. Dinner is served in half Virginian, half French style, in good taste and abundance. No wine is put on the table until the cloth is removed.

In conversation, Mr. Jefferson is easy and natural, and apparently not ambitious; it is not loud, as challenging general attention, but usually addressed to the person next to him. The topics, when not selected to suit the character and feelings of his auditor, are those subjects with which his mind seems particularly occupied; and these, at present, may be said to be science and letters, and especially the University of Virginia, which is coming into existence almost entirely from his exertions, and will rise, it is to be hoped, to usefulness and credit under his continued care. When we were with him, his favorite subjects were Greek and Anglo-Saxon, historical recollections of the times and events of the Revolution, and of his residence in France from 1783–4 to 1789.

"Memorandum of Mr. Jefferson's Conversations," *Private Correspondence of Daniel Webster,* ed. Fletcher Webster (Boston, 1857), 1:364–66.

1. Shoes laced up above the ankles, under pantaloons, were given Jefferson's name because they became popular when he was president.

A Professor Meets the Father of the University

GEORGE LONG, a Cambridge scholar, was the first professor of ancient languages in the University of Virginia. The youngest of the professors recruited abroad, he was among the first to arrive in Charlottesville, several months before the institution opened its doors to students. Jefferson, no mean classicist himself, found Long both able and amiable. Many years later, long after his return to England, the professor recalled his brief but memorable association with Jefferson in a letter to a former student, Henry Tutwiler, the distinguished Alabama educator.

Portfield, Chichester,
May, 30/75. Very Cold.

MY DEAR FRIEND:

I send you a few words at your request, which you may use as you please.

Early in December 1824 I travelled from Washington to Fredericksburg, where I stayed all night. I do not know how I was known, but a gentleman called on me, and asked me to his house, and I spent a pleasant evening. I saw some young Virginian ladies there and I thought they were very charming. I was amused with the curiosity which my new friends showed to hear some news about England. A gentleman came up to me, and asked how I left Mr. Campbell, the poet. Luckily I had lately called on him in London on some business about a relative of his who thought of emigrating to America, and I could therefore give a satisfactory answer. At Fredericksburg I first tasted corn bread, and I used it all the time that I lived in Virginia. I wish that I could have it now.

From Fredericksburg I had a two days' rather unpleasant journey to Charlottesville in the stage coach. The roads were bad, the accommodation not good, and the company very indifferent. The young men of the present day can hardly conceive what this road was then, for I suppose that there is now a railroad the whole distance.

At Charlottesville, I mean of course the University near it, I lived at least two months in the house which was assigned to me, in great solitude and during bad weather. It would have been still worse, if I had not experienced the kindness of the Proctor, Mr. Brockenbrough, whose wife's sister I afterwards married. The other professors had embarked in an English vessel for Norfolk, and they had a very long passage. The ship was described to me as something like an old hay stack: it could just float and go before the wind. I had more wisely embarked in one of the New York American packets from Liverpool. Since that time the English have learned to build good ships for the American trade. When my brother professors arrived at the University, they found me eating corn bread and already a Virginian in tastes and habits. Things were rather rough, but I have always had and still have the faculty of making myself happy under any circumstances.

A few days after my arrival at Charlottesville, I walked up to Monticello to see Mr. Jefferson. I made myself known to his servant, and was introduced into his great room. In a few minutes a tall dignified old man entered, and after looking at me a moment said, Are you the new professor of antient languages? I replied that I was. He observed, You are very young: to which I answered, I shall grow older. He smiled, and said, That was true. He was evidently somewhat startled at my youthful and boyish appearance; and I could plainly see that he was disappointed. We fell to talking and I stayed to dine with him. He was grave and rather cold in his manner, but he was very polite; and I was pleased with his simple Virginian dress, and his conversation free from all affectation. I remember this interview as well as if it took place yesterday.

During my solitary residence before the University opened I visited Monticello several times and occasionally passed the night there. I thought that he became better satisfied with the boy professor; and we talked on all subjects. He saw that I took great interest in the geography of America and in the story of the revolution; and he told me much about it, but in a very modest way as to himself. He showed me the original draft of the Declaration of Independence; and he could clearly see that I was in habits, as I have always been and still am, a man who preferred plain republican institutions to the outward show and splendour of European kingdoms—when I say "republican institution," I mean genuine republican, for a republic may have the name, and very little besides that I value.

I often saw Mr. Jefferson between this time and his death. When he came on his horse to the University, he generally called on me. His thoughts were always about this new place of education of which he was really the founder; and though the first few years of the University were not quite satisfactory, he confidently looked forward to the future and to the advantages which the state would derive from the young men who were educated in the University of Virginia.

I remember well a long conversation which I once had with Mr. Jefferson on George Washington. He spoke of him freely and generously, as a man of great and noble character. Mr. [George] Tucker in his life of Jefferson has given the character of George Washington as Jefferson wrote it; and it is perhaps certain that the character was written at the time when Mr. Jefferson spoke of Washington to me, though he told me something more than the written character contains, but nothing that is contradictory to it. The character is exceedingly well written, and it proves that as a mere writer Jefferson might have excelled most men of his day.

I discovered that Mr. Jefferson was well acquainted with Polybius, who is not a good writer, but a man of excellent sense and the soundest judgment. The last time that I saw Mr. Jefferson when he was suffering from a complaint which caused his death, he was reading Pliny's letters, and we had some talk about a passage. A few weeks after when I was at the Sweet Springs during the summer vacation, I heard of his death. There was much foolish display on the occasion in Virginia, and some extravagant bombastic orations, one of them by a man whom I knew. Those who had more sense showed their feelings in another way. The man who had done so much for Virginia and the United States was honoured for his services, for his talents, and his grand and simple character. He ought to be revered by all who enjoy the advantage of being educated in his University, and ever remembered as one of the great men whom Virginia has produced. His great deeds are recorded in the epitaph which he wrote for his own tomb.

George Long to Henry Tutwiler, May 30, 1875, *Letters of George Long,* ed. Thomas Fitzhugh (Charlottesville, Va., 1917), 21–24. Reprinted by permission of the Rare Books Division, Special Collections Department, University of Virginia Library.

⚜ 1825 ⚜

A German Prince
Climbs the Mountain

DUKE BERNHARD of Saxe-Weimar-Eisenach, who toured the United States in 1825–26, was a tall robust man, looking like "one of those gigantic Cossacks," according to one observer, and about thirty-five years of age. Following the Valley from Harpers Ferry, he made his crossing of the Blue Ridge some miles north of Charlottesville. His account offers another view of Jefferson in old age and is especially informative on the picture gallery at Monticello. Bernhard's *Travels* was published in English translation in 1828.

ON THE 25TH OF NOVEMBER, we set out for Charlottesville, thirty-two miles distant, passing over the Blue Ridge. The road is through a country little cultivated, and without a single village; and the number of separate houses could scarcely be more than a dozen. After we had gone about five miles, we arrived at the western base of the Blue Ridge, which affords an agreeable view, being overgrown with wood up to the top. Then we entered a narrow valley, and when the road began to ascend, we alighted and walked over the mountains. I was surprised to find the road less steep then I expected, and it was also pretty good. From elevated places, the day being not so foggy as the preceding ones, we had many fine views of the mountains. The wood consisted of oak trees, and different kinds of nut trees; here and there were colossal fir, larch, Weymouth's pine and acacia trees. Evergreen rhododendrons, for which some amateurs in Europe spend a great deal of money, are growing here in abundance, also wild vines, which wind themselves round the trees. The prospect on the mountains would have been more pleasant, had there been some marks of human dwellings, but we saw only two miserable log houses, inhabited by dirty and ragged negro families, on the whole tract for eight miles over the mountains; and we met but a few carts loaded with flour.

Having crossed the Blue Ridge, we arrived at a good-looking country house, and a mill called Brown's Farm, situated at the base of the mountains, and took our dinner there. This house is surrounded by fields belonging to it, and from its piazza there is a very fine view of the mountains. From this place we had yet twenty miles to Charlottesville. The road became less hilly, at least we had no more mountains to cross; however, the road continued very rough, and we were rudely jolted. About eight o'clock in the evening we reached Charlottesville, in which the houses appeared to be scattered. In its vicinity is a new establishment for education, called University of Virginia. The next morning we went to see the university, which is one mile distant from the town. . . .

President Jefferson invited us to a family dinner; but as in Charlottesville there is but a single hackney-coach, and this being absent, we were obliged to go the three miles to Monticello on foot.

We went by a pathway, through well cultivated and enclosed fields, crossed a creek named Rivanna,[1] passing on a trunk of a tree cut in a rough shape, and without rails; then ascended a steep hill overgrown with wood, and came on its top to Mr. Jefferson's house, which is in an open space, walled round with bricks, forming an oblong, whose shorter sides are rounded; on each of the longer sides are portals of four columns.

The unsuccessful waiting for a carriage, and our long walk, caused such a delay, that we found the company at table when we entered; but Mr. Jefferson came very kindly to meet us, forced us to take our seats, and ordered dinner to be served up anew. He was an old man of eighty-six years of age,[2] of tall stature, plain appearance, and long white hair.

In conversation he was very lively, and his spirits, as also his hearing and sight, seemed not to have decreased at all with his advancing age. I found in him a man who retained his faculties remarkably well in his old age, and one would have taken him for a man of sixty. He asked me what I had seen in Virginia. I eulogized all the places, that I was certain would meet with his approbation, and he seemed very much pleased. The company at the table, consisted of the family of his daughter, Mrs. Randolph, and of that of the professor of mathematics at the university,[3] an Englishman and of his wife. I turned the conversation to the subject of the university, and observed, that this was the favourite topic with Mr. Jefferson; he entertained very sanguine hope as to the flourishing state of the university in future, and believed that it, and the Harvard University near Boston, would in a very short time be the only institutions, where the youth of the United States would receive a truly classical and solid education. After dinner we intended to take our leave, in order to return to Charlottesville; but Mr. Jefferson would not consent to it. He pressed us to remain for the night at his house. The evening was spent by the fire; a great deal was said about travels, and objects of natural history; the fine arts were also introduced, of which Mr. Jefferson was a great admirer. He spoke also of his travels in France, and the country on the Rhine, where he was very much pleased. His description of Virginia is the best proof what an admirer he is of beauties of nature. He told us that it was only eight months since he could not ride on horseback; otherwise, he road every day to visit the surrounding country; he entertained, however, hopes of being able to re-commence the next spring his favourite exercise. Between nine and ten o'clock in the evening, the company broke up, and a handsome room was assigned to me.

The next morning I took a walk round the house, and admired the beautiful panorama, which this spot presents. On the left, I saw the Blue Ridge, and between them and Monticello are smaller hills. Charlottesville and the University lay at my feet; before me, the valley of the Rivanna River, which farther on, makes its junction with the James river, and on my right was the flat part of Virginia, the extent of which is lost in distance; behind me was a towering hill, which limited the sight. The interior of the house was plain, and the furniture somewhat of an old fashion. In the entrance was a marble stove with Mr. Jefferson's bust, by Ceracchi. In the rooms hung several copies of the celebrated pictures of the Italian school, views of Monticello, Mount-Vernon, the principal buildings in Washington and Harper's Ferry; there were also an oil painting, and an engraving of the Natural Bridge, views of Niagara by Vanderlin, a sketch of the large picture of Trumbull, representing the surrender at Yorktown, and a pen drawing of Hector's departure, by Benjamin West, presented by him to General

Kosciuszko, finally, several portraits of Mr. Jefferson, among which the best was that in profile by Stuart. In the saloon there were two busts, one of Napoleon as first consul, and another of the Emperor Alexander. Mr. Jefferson admired Napoleon's military talents, but did not love him. After breakfast, which we took with the family, we bid the respectable old man farewell, and set out upon our return on foot to Charlottesville.

Bernhard, Duke of Saxe-Weimar-Eisenach, *Travels in North America in 1825 and 1826* (Philadelphia, 1828), 1:196–99.

1. Probably Moore's Creek.

2. Jefferson was eighty-two at this time.

3. Thomas Key.

~⟨ 1 8 2 6 ⟩~

⟨

A Visit to
the Dying Sage

HENRY LEE, son of the Revolutionary general Light-Horse Harry Lee, was the last visitor to see Jefferson alive. Preparing a new edition of his father's *Memoirs of the War,* young Lee had corresponded with Jefferson regarding that work's harsh view of his conduct as wartime governor of Virginia and had made an appointment to call on him at Monticello. The visit occurred on Thursday, June 29, six days before the master's death. Lee wrote of it in a public letter to the *Richmond Enquirer.*

UPON ARRIVING AT CHARLOTTESVILLE, on the 27th June, although it was reported that Mr. Jefferson was sick, the account seemed neither so definite nor alarming, as to render it proper that I should forego the object of my journey. I therefore, addressed a note to him, signifying my arrival and readiness to await on him next day, or any other day of the week, which might be more agreeable to him. Next morning Mr. Trist[1] called on me, confirmed the account I had before received, and said that Mr. J. had desired that I would dine at Monticello that day or the preceding. The preceding day was the Thursday before his death, and when it came, it seemed to be the general impression around me, that the life of the patriarch was in danger. I therefore, determined to call in the forenoon, and in case his indisposition continued to be serious, to return before dinner to Charlottesville. As I approached the house, the anxiety and distress visible in the countenances of the servants, increased the gloom of my own forebodings, and I entered it under no little agitation. After the object of my early call was made known to Mrs. Randolph, she told me that, although her father had been expecting to see me, he was then too unwell to receive any one. It was but too evident that the fears of his daughter overbalanced her hopes, and while sympathising in her distress, I could not help sighing, to think that, although separated from him only by a thin wall, I was never more to behold the venerable man, who had entered all the walks of politics and philosophy, and in all was foremost—and to whom, the past, and the present, and all future ages are, and will be, so much indebted. However, Mrs. Randolph having left me, to attend to her father, soon returned and observed, that she had taken it for granted that he could not see me; but upon her casually mentioning my arrival, he had desired I should be invited into his chamber. My emotions at approaching *Jefferson's dying bed,* I cannot describe. You remember the alcove in which he slept. There he was extended, feeble, prostrate; but the fine and clear expression of his countenance not all obscured. At the first glance he recognized me, and his hand and voice at once saluted me. The energy of his grasp, and the spirit of his conversation, were such as to make me hope he would yet rally—and that the superiority of mind over matter in his composition, would preserve him yet longer. He regretted that I should find him so helpless—said if he got well, I should see all the papers he had promised. He talked of the freshet which was then prevailing in James River—of its extensive devastation—and said he had never known a more destructive one. He soon, however, passed to the university, expatiated on its future utility—said its cost would not, altogether, exceed 320,000 dollars; commended the professors, and expressed satisfaction at the progress of the students. A sword was suspended at the foot of his bed, which he told me was presented to him by, (I think) an Arabian chief, and that the blade was a true Damascus. At this time he became so cheerful as to smile, even to laughing, at a remark I made. He alluded to the probability of his death—as a man would to the prospect of being caught in a shower—as an event not to be desired, but not to be feared. It was to be apprehended, that the eagerness with which he conversed, would exhaust him, and, therefore, I could not indulge myself with a long interview. Upon promising to withdraw, I observed that I would call to see him again. He said, "well do—but you dine here to-day." To this I replied, "I proposed deferring that pleasure until he got better." He waved his hand and shook his head with some impatience, saying, emphatically—"you *must* dine here—my sickness makes no difference." I consented, left him, and never saw him more. I observed that he kept the flies off himself, and seemed to decline assistance from his attendants. Mrs. Randolph afterwards told me this was his habit—that his plan was to fight old age off, by never admitting the approach of helplessness, and he was, moreover, exceedingly averse to giving trouble. From the interview I conceived strong hopes of his recovering, and when, after dinner, I conversed with his physician, Dr. Dunglison of the university, these hopes were rendered more sanguine. For he seemed to think his disease was conquered, and that he had nothing but the inelastic state of old age to fear. Mrs. Randolph and the family soon appeared to feel the diffusion of these hopes—which were but too fallacious.

I shall never cease to deplore that I did not find him in good health. The rise of the waters, among other disasters, produced this by delaying me.

With great regard, I am, dear sir, faithfully yours.

> H. Lee
> *Washington, 19th August, 1826.*

Letter of Henry Lee, Aug. 19, 1826, in *Niles' Weekly Register*, Nov. 25, 1826.

1. Nicholas P. Trist had married Jefferson's granddaughter Virginia Randolph.

ʔ

Prospects Most Magnificent

THE FAMILY WAS STILL IN RESIDENCE when Henry D. Gilpin, a twenty-six-year-old Philadelphia lawyer, visited Monticello on a tour of Virginia in 1827. A man of letters as well as of the law, he wrote the brief life of Jefferson for John Sanderson's *Biography of the Signers of the Declaration of Independence* and, in 1840, became the first editor of James Madison's writings. Gilpin, with many visitors before and after him, was more enchanted by the natural setting than by the house. His impressions are contained in a letter to his father, which was first published with additional editorial notes in 1968.

THE GREAT OBJECT AT CHARLOTTESVILLE, next, if indeed it is not superior to the University, is Monticello. I had a letter to Mr. Trist, the husband of one of Mr. Jefferson's granddaughters, & now the only gentleman I believe residing there. The ascent to it, is very steep & it is about three miles south east of the town. It is on the summit or point of a hill, which is the last of the various spurs or ridges that run out from the Blue Mountain. The house is on the loftiest point surrounded but not obscured by majestic trees, very extensive, with numerous offices attached to it, but dark & much dilapidated with age & neglect. The principal front towards the east has a large & lofty portico, with a vane above it, and a clock under the pediment; indeed on all hands you are struck with the marks of Mr. Jefferson's attention to objects of science. The hall into which you enter is surrounded by statues[,] busts, paintings, Indian curiosities &c.—the rooms are filled with them also, and many are very beautiful. I saw the ladies of the family only for a few minutes for I had promised Mr. Tucker[1] to return to tea & the afternoon was already considerably advanced; after walking through a few of the principal rooms therefore, which however, was not pleasant, as the family were occupying them, Mr. Trist took me to the family grave yard which is on the midst of a wood & about half a mile from the house—the grave of Mr. Jefferson is on one side still marked by the freshness of the earth & an oak tree hanging over it[;] it is between the tombs of his wife & his brother in law Dabney Carr, a gentleman of high character to whom he was much attached. There is no monument, but a plain obelisk of which he left the design is to be placed over his grave—many of his family are buried around, but with one or two exceptions, their graves are undistinguished except by a board stuck in at the head with the initials painted or cut in it. From this place we walked into the gardens, to see the places where the best views presented themselves, & which Mr. Jefferson had fixed on as favourite spots for walking, reading or reflection. These views are the most extensive I have ever seen in my life; looking to the southwest, your eye runs over a plain bounded all along the right by the Blue Ridge with all its various undulations, and its base sinking into hills & valleys, covered with wood & cultivation; in this direction you see Willis's mountain at the distance of eighty miles and presenting, as Volney[2] told Mr. Jefferson exactly the appearance of the Great pyramids of Egypt seen from that distance; it gives you an idea of the immensity of those structures beyond anything that can be imagined; on a point of the mountain commanding this prospect, there is an eminence where Mr. Jefferson had erected a little Grecian temple & which was a favourite spot with him to read & sit in—we stood on the spot, but a violent storm some years since blew down the temple & no vestiges are left—from here we walked round to the east edge of the mountain in front of the house, where the view extends as far as the eye can reach, over the immense plain which forms the lower part of Virginia, & the boundary of which is only the union of the plain & the horizon in the distance; but of all the prospects I have ever beheld the most magnificent is towards the north & north east— it looks over the tops of several mountains—it has the Blue Mountain again on the left—it embraces hills at the distance of a hundred & twenty miles—while at your feet, you look down on Charlottesville

& the valley around it, the Rivanna winding through it, the University with its domes & scattered houses, & the farms buildings & fields green with tobacco, all so near & so directly beneath you, that it seems as if a stone could be thrown upon any object below—along the north side of the house commanding this prospect is a terrace which was Mr. Jefferson's favourite walk in his later years. He was not, however a great walker, but very fond of riding; until his last illness & within a few weeks of his death, he never omitted his daily ride, his horse which Mr. Trist showed me, is a young & fiery one, but he always went alone, having an extreme repugnance to the attendance of a servant; this latterly led him into some dangerous situations, & once when attempting to ford a stream in the neighbourhood, after he was eighty years of age, the rapidity of the current which had been swollen by the rains, swept him off, & both he & his horse were nearly drowned. Nothing however c[oul]d induce him to do any thing which had the appearance either of dependance or ostentation. Mr. Trist told me many anecdotes of his goodness, his immense application, the arrangement of his time &c. which would fill more space & take more time than I can now afford you, so that you must wait to hear them from my lips. They wished me to remain to tea, but it was already late, & I had to hasten back to the University, which I did not reach till long after dark. I slept very soundly, not "inter sylvas Academi" but in an excellent bed of the professor's—and the next morning made a visit with him all over the institution.

"A Tour of Virginia in 1827: Letters of Henry D. Gilpin to His Father," ed. Ralph D. Gray, *Virginia Magazine of History and Biography* 76 (1968): 466–68. Reprinted by permission.

1. George Tucker was professor of moral philosophy in the University of Virginia and Jefferson's first major biographer.

2. The comte de Volney, the much-traveled French scholar and writer, had visited Jefferson at Monticello in 1796.

A Frigid Tour of
the Desolate House

ANNE ROYALL was a gruff and hardy sixty-year-old widow who had turned to writing travel journals to earn a living. On the cold February day in 1830 when she and her courtly companions took the road to Monticello, Jefferson's grave was but rudely marked and the house, left to caretakers, had been emptied of all that gave it life and dignity. Mrs. Royall's report is full of interesting, though often confusing and erroneous, information; and the crudeness of the tour is more than matched by the gracelessness of her prose. The selection is taken from *Mrs. Royall's Southern Tour.*

THIS WAS SATURDAY; the next day was all I had to spare—the stage leaving Charlottesville early on Monday, so that if I visited *Monticello* at all, it must be done on Sunday. Monticello is two miles from Charlottesville. The weather was exceedingly cold, and snow began to fall; but all this did not discourage me. The only difficulty was, whether any person could be found, hardy enough to face the storm, which appeared to be gathering. I happened to say something of the visit, generally, that evening, and in a short time received the following card, which ought to immortalize South Carolina and Georgia.

Col. B. T. Moseley, of Greensborough, Georgia, and Capt. C. J. Nixon, of Camden, South Carolina, present their compliments to Mrs. Royall, and request the favor of her company, to Monticello, to-morrow. Mrs. Royall will please appoint the hour that may be convenient and agreeable to her feelings.

B. T. Moseley

C. J. Nixon

We would be glad to know, immediately, whether we shall have the honor of your company, in order to make suitable arrangements.

B. T. M.

C. J. N.

Mrs. Royall, Present

Thus, those noble young men ran away with the *laurels* of Virginia, whose son, my husband was, and who served his country the whole of our revolutionary struggle! But while I do justice to those chivalrous young men, I by no means withhold it from Virginia: Mr. Carr was transcendently kind, and devoted every moment of his time to me; so also was Mr. Stockton, the nephew of my friend of the same name, of Baltimore. He not only devoted his time, but offered his Stage and four horses to take me and my friends to Monticello. But the high minded South would hear of no compromise—they hired a Hack, and had everything in readiness by nine o'clock, next morning.

But it was a severe undertaking, being still colder than the previous day, and the snow falling in a shower—I never flinched! It was now or never. The winter was advancing—spring was approaching, I had all the Southern States to visit, including New Orleans; and were I to stop for every snow, I should never accomplish my plan; and we set out, accompanied by Mr. R. A. Springs, a young gentleman, from York, S.C.

We kept the windows closed, and being well wrapped up, we were quite comfortable.

We chatted gaily, and the gentlemen pointed out the different farms and amongst them, that of the son-in-law of Thomas *Man[n]* Randolph, a most delightful situation, and very romantic.

We soon began to rise the mountain, the road passing over a most enchanting stream, which came rushing down the mountain side; we wound our way round the steeps, and gradually conquered them by sloping along their sides, these were bounded by deep vales, intermingled with piles of rocks, rounding hills, and lofty timber, these were

115

again mingled with pines: but the snow began to fall so fast that we were unable to see before us, but the prospect must be one of the finest in the United States.

We approached Monticello, by a sloping pine ridge, the only accessible way to it.

Before we came in sight of the building, we had to open a gate, and here we turned suddenly to the left, still pursuing the ridge.

At length we passed a *pine tree* at the root of which, lies the sage of Monticello! The place was enclosed to some distance round, perhaps an acre: it was a poor spot of ground, with a gentle slope; a few bricks lying loose upon the top of the ground, were pointed out to me at the root of the pine tree, "those bricks" said the gentlemen, "lie at the head of the grave, and are all that mark the remains of Jefferson!" He gave orders that no stone should be placed at his head. It was the burying ground of the family, enclosed by a low, rough stone wall, with a plain, neat gate at the upper end.

A short distance from this, is the summit of the mountain, upon which the Mansion stands.

As we draw near, its white lofty walls and magnificent windows, appeared through the trees which surround it. I was all eye, and turning my head to the left, I discovered the stable, once a pine [fine] building, on my right; the mansion being on my left. It was dropping down throughout, one of the corners had fallen some feet.

From the snow and our ignorance of the way, we had to quit the carriage some distance, and walk to the house, the doors in front and the end, we discovered were not used, and we walked on to the other front, and crossing the court, we knocked at a door which we found open, but receiving no answer, we walked in, and passing through a narrow passage, with a door on each side, both shut, we came to a third door on our left, which stood open, here we found a great coarse Irish woman, sitting by a tolerable fire in a neat room. This woman with her husband, (then absent) were put there to take care of the house: besides herself, there was small child and a stout coarse girl— she offered us chairs, and being very cold, we coaxed her to have more wood laid on the fire, and the gentlemen apprizing her of our business she very readily agreed to show us the rooms for fifty cents.—This I was told was contrary to the orders of the proprietors, who left directions that no stranger should pay for viewing the rooms. This female was not satisfied with this, but when I desired the little girl to bring me a few stalks of a beautiful tall green rush which embellished the shrubberies—she observed "poor thing, she had a good way *till* go for it, and its very cold too"—I gave her 6¼ cents: the girl was ugly, and the woman uglier and sly, and palavering with all.

She first took us into the north front room, which is circular, and not very large: in this, stood a Bust of Mr. Jefferson taken in France, when he was young, and said to be well done: round the top of this room ran a gallery, leaving the centre open.—From this room we turned through a wide opening, south into the dining room: the dining room was small, octagon in shape, with windows from the ceiling to the floor, these were extensive and shed a great light. But the floor was a great curiosity, done in Mosaic, by Dinsemore & Nelson, it consisted of alternate, very bright brown wood, about ten inches, octagon shape, of a spruce of cherry color: this again was empaled with a narrow strip of white, I should think, the border is also octagon, and both of ivory smoothness—these are alternately checkered throughout. The sudden appearance of this novelty, and the brilliancy reflected from the large, long windows, thrown open to favor us with the light, filled me with surprise. There was no furniture in the room with the exception of two massy pier glasses attached to the petition, one on each side of the opening into the round parlor. They were covered with gauze and nearly the size of those in the east room,[1] but much better stuff—they go with the free-hold.

On the right of the dining room, we found the *sitting room,* where the family took tea: this was quite a small room, not larger than chambers of our day: the architecture of this room, for taste, variety and skill, was superior to any I ever met with; the ornamental part of the whole of the interior, including the mantle piece, was new to me, though it was much plainer than I expected.

A door opened from the sitting room into a passage through which the dinner used to be raised from the kitchen, and thence conveyed along the passage into the dining room, this passage was narrow and dark, as were the one we entered at first; there were besides these, four rooms on the lower floor, two on the right and two on the left, those on the right were quite small to those on the left: one was the room in which Mr. Jefferson worked, which it appeared he did, from the appearance of the room, the impliments for working in wood, squares, &c. lying about the room,—the one next to it, was Mr. Jefferson's chamber in which he died: this is kept shut—I saw the bed, however, through the window.

From this we went up stairs into the second story, which consists mostly of chambers, with low windows. The beds in these chambers were not placed on bedsteads, but in recesses made exactly to fit the beds, which were narrow, as appeared from the frames upon which they lay: these frames were about one foot and a half from the floor, and were still in the recesses, with buttons for the cords.

There are twenty rooms in the whole, including those on the lower floor.

The woman was unable to tell us which was the Library, but we supposed it to be a beautiful octagon on the second floor.[2] The architecture of this room was inimitably fine, with three circular windows at the end, of the first workmanship.

In the garret we found Mrs. *Jefferson's spinnet* partly broken, it was the first I ever saw, it has keys something like a piano, but it is much lower, and the frame not so large, and the shape of a harpsichord. It stood amongst heaps of slain coffee-urns, chinaware, glasses, globes, chairs and bedsteads. The stairs in all cases were very narrow, and rather steep, but the marble hearths and the ornamental work of the chimney pieces, were very handsome and fresh. But there was not what we would call a large room in the whole. The beauty of the building however is greatly enchanced by the site upon which it stands. One is astonished at the lofty trees which have taken root and over-spread the surrounding ground: which, though on the summit of a barren mountain is a rich regular plain; the surface being removed and reduced to an even plain, and planted with trees by Mr. Jefferson many years ago, at an infinite expense: the whole comprises several acres of an oblong shape. The trees are of all sorts, very large and flourishing. It does actually look like enchantment, to see such an even, fertile plain, covered with tall trees, with a lofty mansion in the midst, upon the summit of a rugged mountain! The descent at all points except one (the way we went) is abrupt, and the view from it on a fair day, must surpass any view of mountain scenery in the State. But unfortunately, it snowed so fast we were unable to see twenty yards—part of the summit appeared to have been a garden, but hardly a vestige of it remained. The day was so cold, particularly at Monticello, that my hands were so benumbed I was unable to write: from this cause, which I lament, my sketch of Monticello is very short and imperfect; but my own gratification was unspeakably great in seeing a place so celebrated. After walking *to* and *fro,* till we were almost frozen, we assembled once more round the fire, and the woman treated the gentlemen with some very indifferent cider, of which they merely tasted. But their providential politeness surprised me: they had taken the precaution to put a bottle of wine in the pocket of the carriage, lest I might be chilled with the cold, and if I ever had drank wine, I should certainly have pledged those amiable young men, whose gentlemanly attention was beyond all praise.

They had the carriage brought to the door, and we returned on the opposite side from the one we approached.

I was told Mr. Jefferson's farm lay off some distance upon the side of the mountain, or perhaps the plain below: but I saw nothing of it. I understood that Monticello could be seen from Charlottesville on a fair day.

As we descended the mountain, we began to feel warm, and found a still greater change in the air when we reached the village.

Anne Royall, *Mrs. Royall's Southern Tour* (Washington, D.C., 1830), 1:87–91.

1. The mirrors in the East Room of the White House.

2. The dome room on the third floor.

༆

Glorious Landscape—
Noble Ruin

Two and one-half years after Mrs. Royall's tour, the impression of ruin and desolation thickened. John H. B. Latrobe, the son of Benjamin H. Latrobe, the distinguished architect and engineer who had served President Jefferson as superintendent of the federal buildings in Washington, had intended to follow in his father's footsteps but instead became a lawyer and many-sided public servant. He shared his father's taste for the Greek over the Roman style; partly for this reason he found little to admire in the buildings of the University of Virginia and said that the whole had the appearance of incompleteness and neglect. The same, only more so, was true of Monticello. Latrobe waxed lyrical over the landscape observed from the summit, however. He described his visit in a letter later published by his biographer.

I got a horse on my return to the tavern, and started to Monticello, about two and a half miles off, on the summit of the mountain immediately above the Ravenna. It had rained heavily for the last hour. In the afternoon it cleared up cool and bright, then I entered the thick wood around the base of the mountain. A steep and rough road led me to the summit, and on the esplanade formed there, partly by nature and partly by art, was the mansion house and its offices, now the property of a Dr. Barclay. The first thing that strikes you is the utter ruin and desolation of everything. The house is of brick, in the same wretched style as the university, with a portico of four Doric columns on each front and an arcade of brick at the extremities of the wings.

A dome surmounts the whole. Here again the general effect is good, notwithstanding the bad taste of the details. The owner was absent and I could not obtain admittance, but was shown through an open window the room in which Mr. Jefferson died. The internal arrangement, so far as I could judge of it by the peeps I made into peepable places, is whimsical and, according to present notions of country houses, uncomfortable, being cut up into small apartments. On this subject I really am not competent to speak. The roofs of the offices are on a line with the floor of the main building, extend on either side of it, and are turned to the southwest, making the three sides of a parallelogram. They are flat and form a terraced walk. The northwest angle seems to have been a favorite spot of Mr. Jefferson. It is completely shaded by trees and garden chairs are permanently fixed there. The view from it is magnificent. You look across the valley between the southwest mountain and the Blue Ridge, until the high and rolling summits of the latter range form a bold horizon, extending from the south around into the north. Forests and cultivation are here mingled in goodly proportion. The University of Virginia has nestled upon the little eminence and embowering creeks, and nearer the Valley of Charlottesville, which is a pleasant resting place for the eye among the wide fields which surround it. Here and there the Ravenna glitters in the landscape, and the roar of the stream over the dam below rises up gently with a soothing influence. Vast masses of clouds, the remnants of the afternoon gust, are lying about the sun, and take those hues which pen cannot describe nor pencil imitate, and which few but us Americans have seen. Long shadows are stretching themselves further and further towards Monticello, until the disappearance of the sun behind the clouds throws one broad veil over the entire landscape, and the distant mountains take the hue of deeper purple. Then bursting forth again the sun, within a palm's width of the edge of that round, isolated hill, casts its level rays eastward, and the points of all the intermediate eminences glitter like diamonds and momentary lustre another moment, when the broad flood of mellow light westward along indicates that the sun has been there, and almost compensates by its beauty for the sun's departure. Would that you could see Monticello to advantage as I did, and watch the sun as it sets behind those glorious mountains. Northward and southward from the Esplanade, you see the mountains of this particular ridge, and eastward your eye roams over an unlimited and rolling forest, save where to the north-east a bit of cultivation appears along the base of the Southwest mountain. Take it all in all, Monticello is a spot on which one might well be contented to dwell in the silence and solitude of its lofty summit, above the contentions and meannesses and inconsistencies of his fellow men and gaze down upon this world which they inhabit, having his mind elevated by its glorious perfection to his Creator and Judge. The old philosopher who last inhabited it, despite his errors, and he had many both as a man and as a statesman, possessed too many of the attributes of real greatness, in his bold conceptions and firm, undeviating purposes, not to be worthy of this noble spot which he had selected and improved; and when his spirit took its flight from it, there remained a halo lingering around it, which has made it a monument to his memory. As such I visited it, and as such it will be visited until the history of America shall cease to exercise an influence upon the conduct of its people.

I certainly did not expect to find at Monticello anything which would give rise to feeling, wholly personal to myself. Yet so it was. Singularly enough at the corner of the terrace before mentioned and overlooking Charlottesville, and in the centre of the square surrounded by the garden chairs, which I have already told you were fixed there, I saw a pedestal, deprived of that which the iron bolt projecting from its centre proved to have once belonged there. Not far off, however, I saw the capital of the column, somewhat mutilated, which had been thrown or fallen down from the pedestal, and recognized at first glance a capital of the order of architecture invented by my father during Mr. Jefferson's administration, in which the place usually occupied by Acanthus leaves of the Corinthian columns is filled by ears of corn, grouped together with due regard to beauty in their proportions. You see it in the vestibule of the North Wing of the Capitol at Washington. You may not perfectly understand my feelings, and may smile at my mentioning such a trifle. But to think that this spot, visited by thousands in the life of Mr. Jefferson, contained something that recalled my parent's genius, caused a current of pleasant feeling to pass through my bosom, and with a sort of filial reverence I moved the stone from the wreck of the garden chair on which it had fallen and placed it upright. I know you are laughing at all this, but truly my poor father met in this world so little of that favor of reward or appreciation that much inferior qualities have won for other men, that I treasure up after his death anything that looks like a tribute to him, however trifling.

Before I left Monticello I took a sketch of the building looking North, which I will show you upon my return.

John E. Semmes, *John H. B. Latrobe and His Times, 1803–1891* (Baltimore, 1917), 248–51.

7

Monument of
an Unbeliever

NOT EVERYONE who went to Monticello was an admirer of Thomas Jefferson. A prominent clergyman, the Reverend Stephen Higginson Tyng, made his visit while in Charlottesville to attend a convention of the Reformed Episcopal church in the spring of 1840. In his eyes Jefferson was an infidel subverter of Christianity. And for all its "outward magnificence," Monticello in decay was a fitting monument of "the man who set himself against the Lord of Hosts." His report was published in the church newspaper, the *Episcopal Recorder,* in Philadelphia. The local citizenry, who were implicated in Tyng's opinions of Jefferson's character, were indignant and called a meeting which adopted resolutions renewing the community's testament of esteem at the time of Jefferson's retirement in 1809.

Charlottesville, Va., May 27, 1840.
DEAR BRETHREN, —The continuance of an easterly storm has kept me here, since the convention adjourned. I parted with all my brethren on Monday, separating to their various parishes and homes. It was a melancholy and painful day. The streets of this village, which had been so thronged with company, appeared peculiarly empty and desolate, and the houses which had been pouring out their guests every day as we passed by, seemed to be all shut up in mourning, after the early hours of Monday had gone. I believe there has been no other clergyman of our church than myself in the town since. There are two points of interest to me in my visit here, to which I will devote this letter, de-

signing to write no other till I am on my journey from hence to the mountains. The one is my visit to Monticello, the residence of Mr. Jefferson; the other is the university which he established. My visit to the former was made on an afternoon of last week with a lady well known in the literary world, and worthy to be known much more widely, who had been for many years an inmate of Mr. Jefferson's family, to which she is a relative.[1] After dinner at the university where I happened to be that day with her, she gave me the invitation to join a party she was about escorting to Monticello. The place is now owned and occupied by Captain Levy, of the United States Navy, who probably has been so troubled with the frequency of visits to his dwelling, that he has the reputation of being averse to receiving company to his house. It was therefore an object to be under the patronage of a member of Mr. J.'s family, to whom it is understood the doors are always open. The house is upon the summit of a mountain about three miles from Charlottesville. The afternoon was clear, and well adapted to our purpose, and the ride was an extremely pleasant one. The ascent to the mountain is by a road which has been well cut out and graduated on the mountain side, through the midst of a wood which completely hides everything from your view, save in a single spot, until you reach the very summit, and then a prospect bursts upon your eyes more magnificent than I had ever conceived, and certainly unsurpassed by any thing on earth. When we reached the top of the mountain, which has been levelled and cleared at an expense beyond present knowledge or calculation, the whole scene completely entranced me. The house and out-buildings I left unnoticed, until I had walked in solitude around the brow of the hill, which is the edge of the lawn surrounding the house, and contemplated the grandeur of the scene before me. The views are divided into two main ones. The western view extends over a section of the most fertile and varied country, covered with plantations, interspersed with groves and cultivated fields, ornamented with highly finished and beautiful residences, and presenting so many and so great a variety of objects, that the eye is bewildered in the discrimination of them, and is satisfied only by a regular examination of the successive points which are presented. The village of Charlottesville with the splendid buildings of the university, lie on the left almost under you; you look down upon them as a little cluster of houses over which you might spread a mantle as they sleep beneath your feet. The highly cultivated hills of Albemarle, mingled with the residences of their wealthy population, extend beyond, and to the right. The Ravenna river with its green skirted banks winding through the valleys like a silver stream, beheld at intervals as it starts from among and around the hills quite in the distance, and flowing on until it seems lost in the very mountain on which you stand, and around the base of which it flows, forms a beautiful feature in the landscape. Beyond the counties of Madison and Rappahanock, extend the variety and splendour of the view to an undefined distance. The whole prospect is bounded by the Blue Ridge, which stretches off towards the north, and which Mr. Jefferson estimated might be seen for near a hundred miles in its extent. The summits of these mountains form the horizon, cast into every shape of beauty, clothed with the haziness which has given, I suppose, the designation to the ridge, and impressing the idea of great sublimity upon the mind. You stand and trace out this irregularly curving horizon, until it fades away in the distant north, perhaps sixty or eighty miles from your own position. The whole scene is magnificent in the highest degree. How could an intelligent mind abide and dwell with the witness of this glory before it day by day, and fail to offer the acknowledgement and homage to the great Being whose hand had formed the whole? The eastern view is of a different description, less varied, perhaps less beautiful, but having peculiar and great attractions. Beneath, you see the Ravenna again as it comes from under the mountain, and flows on in a southern direction to its junction with the James River. There is a large and handsome manufactory upon it just before you, which, connected with the cluster of houses around it, and encompassed in the green woods, forms a beautiful point. Beyond, the country seems to stretch out in a vast level of woods, in which there are no important elevations, save in one point to the distant horizon. This view spreads over Fluvanna county, of which Mr. Jefferson used to say, if it could be but converted into a lake would complete entirely the beauty of the prospect. There is a want of some sheet of water to perfect the scene. Beyond this in one point you see the summits of Willis' mountain, at a distance of about sixty miles, which seem to rise upwards in solitude to the sky, as if they were parts of some other land far distant. There is great calmness and quietness resting upon this view. All is in a state of repose, and the eye dwells upon it with great delight. Hours might

be spent in walking around the lawn to survey each portion of the
magnificent panorama with great pleasure. I regretted the little time I
had to cast my eye about, compelled me rapidly and imperfectly to
notice a view so worthy of long contemplation. But I rejoiced in the
reflection as I surveyed the glorious scene, "these are thy works, Parent
of good." God is seen reigning in his power in such an exhibition of
the works of his hand. I rejoiced in the reflection, that redemption has
brought that glorious Creator so near to his sinful creatures, and that
as I beheld what God could do, I might also say, "this God is our God
for ever and ever." How precious becomes the appropriation of such
a Being as the portion of the redeemed soul! From the contemplation
of the outward magnificence we turned to examine the house of a man
who lived and died an unbeliever amidst all that God had thus given
him. It was undoubtedly an elegant mansion, though now extremely
dilapidated. We found the owner very polite, and ready to welcome us
to a view of the premises. It would be vain to describe the mansion. It
is a fanciful, irregular brick building of one apparent story, though
having a low second story, I believe, surmounted with a dome. It is
composed of a large number of rooms of all shapes and sizes, though
without one room that could be singly called an elegant one among
the whole. The hall you enter is handsome; beyond it is a drawing-
room with a highly polished tesselated floor of beech and cherry
wood, which is truly beautiful. The dining-rooms on one side, and
Mr. Jefferson's study on the other, complete the habitation. The latter
was composed of five rooms, which in his time were always kept
locked. Our friend who was guiding us, showed the door at which
every one who desired admission there knocked for an entrance. His
bed, in a low alcove between two rooms, still remains in its position.
This, with some mirrors, constitutes the remnant of his furniture,
which is there to be seen. I cast a hasty glance around, but I felt no
interest in the scene. All that was to be beheld there were, as their
highest charm, but monuments of a man who spent his life in oppos-
ing the cause most dear to my heart, and in which my interests for
eternity are all involved. I had no respect for him while living, and
every view of his character and influence since his death has increased
my abhorrence of them. I was glad to leave the secne within, and
return to that without. On my way down the mountain I went to the
burial ground of the family. A single low obelisk of granite without a

name covers the spot where Jefferson's mortal remains are lying. Everything is ruin around. The brick wall is torn down to its foundations, the tombstone itself has been broken and marred in every line and corner, I suppose by devotees who would carry away a memento of his name. To my eye the battered, defaced, and broken stone, appeared but an illustration of the character of him whom it commemorates, as it now appears in the eyes of men, while the desolation around would exhibit the ruin and darkness he would have spread upon the world abroad. It was a suitable commemoration of the man who set himself against the Lord of hosts. But his influence has passed away. I have never heard his name spoken with so little respect, and so much aversion, as in this very neighbourhood in which he lived and died. I had never conceived his character so bad as I have found it here. His plans are all defeated. The religion of Jesus triumphs over all his opposition. The university which he founded to overthrow this blessed system has passed from influence, and is likely to be a powerful and permanent instrument to build up what he designed it should destroy. . . . Great as he might have been as a statesman and a philosopher, of which I do not speak, all his greatness has perished and is forgotten because he was an infidel. One cannot listen to all that I have heard and seen without perceiving how self-destructive are the mightiest talents when perverted into opposition to the living God. Nor can the mind forget in such a connection the solemn imprecation of the Scripture, "So let all thine enemies perish, O Lord." I intended to have spoken of the university also in this letter, but I must leave it for another.

Yours affectionately,

S. H. T.

Letter of the Reverend Stephen Higginson Tyng, in the *Episcopal Recorder*, June 13, 1840.

1. The lady has not been identified.

ᴧ 1841 ᴩ

7

An Englishman Finds Beauty amidst Desecration

AMONG THE HOST of English travelers in the antebellum years, James Silk Buckingham was one of the most observant. A man of middle age, who had performed variously as a sea captain, journalist, and member of Parliament, he traveled and lectured extensively in the United States. A great admirer of Jefferson, Buckingham was astonished by the desecration of his tomb—a matter that would finally be rectified by an act of Congress in 1882—and he did not approve of Captain Levy's incongruous additions to the mansion. Buckingham's account was published in his book, *The Slave States of America,* in 1842.

WE LEFT THE HOTEL AT W[e]yer's Cave at nine A.M., on the 16th of August, for Waynesborough, where we arrived at one o'clock: and dining there, we left it at three for Charlottesville, by the mail. Our road lay over a comparatively low portion of the Blue Ridge, in a part called the Rock-fish Gap, the elevation of which was not more than 300 feet above the level of the valley. We wound our way up this amidst a heavy storm of thunder, lightning, and rain, which, while it occasioned us some inconvenience from the imperfect protection which all American coaches afford against the elements, added something to the grandeur of the mountain-scenery. The storm abated, however, before we reached the highest part of the Gap, and the atmosphere becoming clear, we had a splendid and extensive view from the summit; the mountain-ridges of the west being visible in succession, to a distance of seventy or eighty miles, and the broad plains below us to the east, extending the horizon to an equal distance in that direction: the latter resembling the beautiful view from the summit of Catskill Mountain on the Hudson river, from the great abundance of cleared land intermingled with the forest patches of the surface. We lingered to enjoy this splendid view, as it was the last opportunity we should probably ever possess of dwelling with delight upon the mountain-landscapes of this noble State; and when we turned the brow of the Blue Ridge, to wind down its eastern face, we took our last gaze with a feeling of admiration, mingled with regret.

The descent of this mountain-barrier brought us, by several smaller ridges, at length, to the lower plain. . . . The difference of temperature was very perceptible to our feelings when we reached the plain, the air being not only warmer, but heavier, and more humid, so that we experienced a very disagreeable change by the transition. This Blue Ridge is the first great mountain barrier met with in coming up from the sea-coast on the east; and it is the geographical boundary between the two great divisions of the State into Eastern and Western Virginia. We found here, besides the marked change of temperature, two other corresponding changes;—one, the more frequent cultivation of the tobacco-plant; and the other, the greater abundance of negroes.

There was a marked difference also in the condition of the lands, and in the style and mode of husbandry; everything in this respect was greatly inferior here, to what we had witnessed in the midland region above. Slave-labour, and the cultivation of tobacco, have each had their share in producing this deterioration. This was observed by Mr. Jefferson more that fifty years ago; for in his Notes on Virginia, when speaking of the extensive production of tobacco, of which no less than 70,000 hogsheads were grown in this State in the year, 1758, he says—

> But the western country on the Mississippi, and the midlands of Georgia, having a better sun, will be able to undersell these two States (Maryland and Virginia), and will oblige them to abandon the raising of tobacco altogether. And a happy obligation for them it will be. It is a culture productive of infinite wretchedness. Those employed in it are in a continued state of exertion beyond the powers of nature to support. Little food of any kind is raised by them, so that the men and ani-

mals on these farms are badly fed, and the earth is rapidly impoverished. The cultivation of wheat is the reverse in every circumstance. Besides clothing the earth with herbage, and preserving its fertility, it feeds the labourers plentifully, requires from them only a moderate toil, except in the season of harvest, raises great numbers of animals for food and service, and diffuses plenty and happiness among the whole. It is easier to make a hundred bushels of wheat than a thousand weight of tobacco, and they are worth more when made.

These opinions of Mr. Jefferson were published in Virginia as long ago as 1786, and considering the high rank, great reputation, and unbounded popularity of their author, one might have hoped that they would have changed the current of public opinion on this subject, and led to the speedy abandonment of so pernicious a culture; but no such result has yet taken place, nor has the competition of the newer States yet effected the object of driving the production from Maryland and Virginia, as Mr. Jefferson anticipated. Like the madness of converting grain, which Nature has given for wholesome food, by the process of distillation, into poisonous spirits, which is practised to so great an extent in all the countries of Europe, this devotion of lands in America, so well adapted to yield sustenance for man, to the cultivation of the poisonous weed tobacco, is one of the strongest perversions of God's best gifts to the worst of purposes; and the process by which this is effected is as disgusting as the result is degrading and deplorable. . . .

After a pleasant ride of five hours from Waynesborough, going a distance of twenty-six miles, we reached Charlottesville at eight in the evening, and took up our quarters at the Eagle Hotel.

On the following day, August 17, we made a pleasant party with our Baltimore friends, to visit Monticello, the residence of the late Mr. Jefferson, and the site of his tomb, as well as to see the University of Virginia, of which he was the founder, both being within a short distance of Charlottesville.

Winding our way to the south-east from Charlottesville, we crossed a deep valley, and ascended a steep hill, about 500 feet in height, near the summit of which we first came to the tomb of Jefferson; the neglected and wretched condition of which ought to make every American, who values the Declaration of his country's Independence, blush with shame. If the illustrious ex-President had been the contriver of a treasonable plot for the subjugation or enslavement of his country, instead of one of its most distinguished patriots and deliverers, his sepulchre could not be more entirely abandoned. It was at his own desire that his interment should be simple, and his monument plain, and this was in perfect accordance with his republican principles and practice; but this is no excuse whatever for the shameful indifference or neglect of his survivors, in permitting it to be what it now is, a perfect wreck, though little more than ten years have elapsed since his death. As at present seen, the small enclosure, not more than from forty to fifty feet square, had its stone-wall half dilapidated, its wooden gate of entrance broken and unhung, its interior grown over with rank straggled weeds: the simple granite obelisk standing over Mr. Jefferson's remains, chipped at all the angles by persons carrying off relics; the marble slab that contained the inscription, directed by himself to be placed there, taken away, and the hollow space which contained it left void in the front of the obelisk; the marble slab which covered the tomb of his wife close beside the obelisk broken in two, and large portions of one of the broken halves carried away; in short, the whole place in a state of complete abandonment and disorder.

We ascended from hence, by a short road, to the summit of the hill, and came at length to the platform of lawn, in the centre of which is seated the house, which, for many years, was Mr. Jefferson's dwelling. A very graphic and faithful description of this is given in Wirt's Eulogy on Adams and Jefferson, a portion of which is worth transcribing.

> *The Mansion House at Monticello was built and furnished in the days of Mr. Jefferson's prosperity. In its dimensions, its architecture, its arrangements, and ornaments, it is such a one as became the character and fortune of the man. It stands upon an elliptic plain, formed by cutting down the apex of the mountain; and to the west, stretching away to the north and the south, it commands a view of the Blue Ridge for 150 miles, and brings under the eye one of the boldest and most beautiful horizons in the world; while on the east it presents an extent of prospect bounded only by the spherical form of the earth, in which Nature seems to sleep in eternal repose, as*

if to form one of her finest contrasts with the rude and rolling grandeur of the west. From this summit, the philosopher was wont to enjoy that spectacle, among the sublimest of Nature's operations, the looming of the distant mountains; and to watch the motion of the planets, and the greater revolutions of the celestial sphere. From this summit, too, the patriot could look down with uninterrupted vision upon the wide expanse of the world around, for which he considered himself born: and upward to the open and vaulted heaven, which he seemed to approach, as if to keep him continually in mind of his high responsibility. It is a scene fit to nourish those great and high-souled principles which formed the elements of his character, and was a most noble and appropriate post for such a sentinel over the rights and liberties of men.

To the truth and beauty of all this, as far as it regards the description of the scene, I yield my ready and hearty assent; but when I read a preceding portion of this eulogy, in which, when speaking of Mr. Jefferson's attachment to Monticello as his home, the orator asks, "Can anything be indifferent to *us*, which was so dear to *him?*" I felt a very strong desire to have these words engraved on a marble tablet, and placed at the entrance to his neglected cemetery, or in the socket of the granite obelisk, from which the inscription dictated by Mr. Jefferson's own hand has been so sacreligiously torn. I fear, however, that it would be lost labour and time; for a people who can boast so much of their public men, when themselves and their country are to be indirectly flattered by their praise, and who do so little to honour their memories and their tombs, when their earthly labours are closed, could not be made sensible to shame by appeals to their justice or reason.

We had some difficulty in obtaining an entrance into the house, as it was in the occupation of a family very little disposed to encourage the visits of strangers. The present proprietor is a Captain Levy, of the United States Navy, now absent on duty in the West Indies. He is by birth and religion a Jew, was a common sailor before the mast in the merchant service, rose to be a mate, was admitted from the merchant service into the Navy, and is now a captain. He is reputed to be very rich, but the present condition of Monticello would not lead the visitor to suppose that it was the property of a person either of taste or munificence. It appears that at the period of his buying it, the house and grounds had become as dilapidated as the tomb, and the roads broken up and destroyed, in which state indeed, they all still remain, for nothing has been done apparently to improve either; but in this condition he purchased the house, the grounds, and 200 acres of farming land, for 2,500 dollars, or 500 [pounds]. sterling,—a sum which any English person would think moderate for a single year's rental of the whole. He is aware, however, that this was a great bargain; for he has since refused 12,000 dollars for the purchase, and fixes 20,000 dollars as its value.

Having obtained admission to the house we found its interior in a better condition than we had expected. The plan is more showy than convenient, everything being sacrificed to the hall, the drawing-room, and the library; the taste is rather French than English, Mr. Jefferson having resided for a long time in Paris, but it is decidedly good taste; and we thought we had not seen any interior of an American residence in the South, better finished or in more harmonious proportions than this. Inlaid diagonal oak floors, lofty rooms, deep recesses, and appropriate fixtures and furniture, all harmonised well together, and left nothing incongruous among what belonged to the mansion in Mr. Jefferson's time. The present proprietor, however, had made some additions, which were not in the same good keeping. For instance, on first entering the hall, we saw on the right, affixed to the wall like a picture, the identical marble tablet which was taken from Jefferson's tomb; and which, here, in the hall of his abode while living, contained this inscription, "Here lies buried, Thomas Jefferson, Author of the Declaration of Independence, and of the Statute for Religious Freedom, and Founder of the University of Virginia." [1] Not far from this was an oil painting, containing a full-length portrait of Captain Levy, in his naval uniform, on the quarter deck of his ship; and in the same room a small lithograph of the same individual, as boatswain's-mate, with his boatswain's call in his hand, leaning on a quarter-deck gun, and with full trousers and flowing cravat, in true boatswain's mate's style. Not far from this was a lithograph portrait of the celebrated rich banker of Philadelphia, Stephen Girard; and both these prints were without frame or glass and merely pinned up against the wall. Other incongruities of evidently recent introduction, were strewed around; but among the relics of its better days, were some good paintings, as well as a full-length statue of Mr. Jefferson,[2] and a good bust of Voltaire.

On retiring from the house, we sat for some time in the Doric portico, which is in excellent taste, and has the very useful additions of a compass inserted in the ceiling above, and a clock in the pediment in front, so that the bearing of every object in the horizon may be easily known. We enjoyed the view from hence greatly, and still more so the extensive and beautiful panorama which is seen from the lawn that surrounds the dwelling, and in which are several beautiful oaks and weeping willows, planted by Mr. Jefferson's own hands. To the south-west, the plain is level, and boundless as the sea. To the north-west, the town of Charlottesville, and the University of Virginia at a little distance from it are each full in sight. At the foot of the hill, which is 500 feet elevated above the plain, flows the Ravenna river, leading on to its navigable point, called the Piraeus, within about a mile of Charlottesville, and ultimately going into the James river, on which Richmond is seated. A noble barrier of mountains forms the back ground of the extensive plain, stretching out in this direction from north to west; and the happy admixture of cultivated openings, with the woodlands intervening, make it as beautiful as it is grand.

We returned to Charlottesville by the same road; and though much fatigued by the hills and the hot sun, we went after dinner to see the University, which lies at a short distance from the town.

James S. Buckingham, *The Slave States of America* (London, 1842), 2:393–403.

1. The crafters of the tombstone, erected seven years after Jefferson's death, followed his instructions to the letter in all respects but one. The epitaph, it was found, could not be cut into the face of the granite obelisk, as Jefferson had directed, and so was inscribed on a marble plaque set into the face. The original tombstone as well as the plaque, still separated from it, are at the University of Missouri in Columbia.

2. Presumably this was the model of the bronze by the French sculptor David d'Angers, which Levy had commissioned and presented to Congress in 1834. When Congress declined the gift, the statue was placed before the White House, and it remained there for many years.

"The Empty Offerings of Laudable Curiosity"

BENSON J. LOSSING, the popular historian and wood engraver of the Civil War era, reached a large audience with an illustrated article on Monticello in *Harper's New Monthly Magazine* in 1853. Like Buckingham before him, he drew upon William Wirt's description of the place; indeed, Lossing's account throughout bears comparison to Buckingham's a decade earlier. The interior furnishings were Levy's rather than Jefferson's, of course. The commodore escorted Lossing through the house.

WHILE THE Author of the Declaration of Independence yet lingered in his glorious retreat from the turmoils of public life, in the quiet bosom of Central Virginia, the saloon and the table at Monticello almost daily received guests from far and near, who came to make the obeisance of reverent admiration and affectionate regard to the Patriot and Sage. Noblemen of every degree—noblemen by kingly patent or hereditary right—noblemen knighted by the touch of public opinion in its awards for intellectual achievements, and noblemen in homely guise of mind and person, but lofty patriotism—all flocked to Monticello, not to bow to the rising sun with selfish orisons, but to pay grateful homage to its beneficence, while the splendors of its declining hours yet illumined this western horizon. . . .

Now the scene is changed. For almost thirty years the mortality of THOMAS JEFFERSON has reposed under the mould, in the margin of the grand old forest which wraps the northwestern slopes of Monticello in its solemn shadows. Of all those who once listened to the music of his voice, and followed with delighted vision the sweep of his finger as he pointed to the magnificent mountains, the rolling plains garnished by the tiller's hand, the winding river, and the vast expanse of woods and fields which spread out in panoramic beauty and grandeur around Monticello, few now remain to charm the generation of to-day with reminiscential narratives. Like the Great Patriot, their bodies are earthed, their spirits are enskied, and their experiences have become traditional or historic. The idol is removed, and the tooth of time has marred the beauty of the shrine. Yet pilgrimages thither have not entirely ceased. The motives which prompt the journey are unlike those of former years; now the worshiper bears only the empty offerings of laudable curiosity. For this no harsh word should be spoken, for such motives are harmless. But too often the curious visitor departs with the guilt of sacrilege upon his soul, with Vandal hand he frequently defaces some fair specimen of the Patriot's taste, and even breaks fragments from the granite obelisk over his grave. In many a private cabinet are "relics from Monticello;" a fragment from the monument, a splinter from the delicately-carved cornice, a brick from the foundation, or a piece of putty from a window-pane, broken, perhaps, during the absence of the owner, to procure it! The sight of these should make the possessors blush for shame, for of all petty thieving, this seems the meanest, and without excuse. Such depredators should be regarded with a contempt akin to hatred.

Prompted by the laudable curiosity alluded to, I turned aside at Richmond, while journeying southward, and visited Monticello in blustery March, when the buds were just bursting, and the blue birds were singing their first carols in the hedges. No longer compelled to traverse the hills and valleys along the James River and the muddy Rivanna, on horseback or in chaise, as in former times, I entered the railway coach at sunrise with the assurance of seeing Monticello at meridian, after sweeping across the chief tributary of the Pamunkey, and traversing a country of varied aspect for more than thirty leagues. Rain was falling copiously. A few miles from Richmond we encountered a freight-train off the track, and the locomotive half-buried in mud. We were compelled to walk a plank, and flounder twenty rods along a narrow causeway through yellow-clay almost ankle deep, to another train beyond, or return to the city. As Americans never retrograde, the ladies gathered up their skirts, and the gentlemen walked as daintily as cats among eggs, to the coach in waiting. Soon all was forgotten, except by a poor fellow who volunteered his assistance to a young woman "walking the plank," when his gallantry and comfort both ended in the ditch below, into which he slipped, and filled a boot with as much mire as his leg would allow. The young lady (fie upon her!) more than smiled upon him, and with due independence helped herself along the muddy dyke, and into the best seat in the car beyond the wreck. The victim cursed the girl, the ditch, and the railway, with great unction. The pert girl made the unchristian excuse for her giggle in his hour of peril: "I didn't *ask* him to help me!"

Within an hour after passing the Junction, in Hanover County, we left the flat country and penetrated the more fertile and hilly region of Louisa and Albemarle, lying along the base of the Southwest Mountain. At Cobham station, we had a glimpse of the residence[1] of the Hon. William C. Rives, our minister to the French Court; and soon afterward reached the Shadwell Station, on the Rivanna, close by the picturesque old mill, once owned by Mr. Jefferson. From this point we had a fine view of Monticello looming up on the southwest, and caught slight glimpses of the white columns of the portico of the mansion on the summit. The clouds had now broken, and all over the thoroughly saturated earth myriads of water-pools glittered in the sun.

I arrived at Charlottesville, in time for dinner, after which, in company with the courteous Editor of one of the village papers (Mr. Cochran), I visited Monticello. The road is very sinuous, especially after fording Moore's Creek. For some distance it courses along the margin of a deep, wooded ravine scooped out from the gap between Monticello and Carter's Mountain. The latter is a portion of the same range of hills, with Monticello (called the Southwest mountain), which dwindle into knolls near the James River, and is memorable in history as the place to which Jefferson fled when Tarleton attempted to capture him, in 1781. At the summit of the gap we passed through a rustic gate and up a winding, stony road, by the grave yard on the skirt of the wood, where rest the mortal remains of the AUTHOR OF THE DECLARATION OF INDEPENDENCE. It is surrounded by a high brick wall, with an iron gate near the road. Just within the gate is the Patriot's grave, over which is a granite monument, eight feet in height, shamefully mutilated by thieving visitors. In the southern face of the pedestal was a marble tablet, with the following inscription, written by the Statesman himself, and found among his papers after his death:

HERE LIES BURIED
THOMAS JEFFERSON:
AUTHOR OF THE DECLARATION OF AMERICAN
INDEPENDENCE,
OF THE STATUTE OF VIRGINIA FOR RELIGIOUS FREEDOM,
AND FATHER OF THE UNIVERSITY OF VIRGINIA.

This tablet has been taken from the monument and placed in the mansion, out of the reach of depredators.

Upon each of the sides of the monument is a grave, covered with a marble slab. One (on the right) is that of his wife, *Martha,* who died in 1782, ten years after their marriage. It had the usual record, and below it are inscribed the following Greek lines:

Εἰ δὲ ϛανόντων περ καταλήθοντ' εἰν' Ἀίδαο,
Αὐτὰρ ἐγω κιαηκεῖθι φιλου μεμνήσομ'
ἑταίρου.

These lines are from the speech of Achilles over the dead body of Hector, in which, after saying he will never forget Patroclus while he has life, adds: "And though spirits in a future state be oblivious of the past, he will even there remember his beloved companion." The other two graves are those of his favorite daughter Martha Wayles Randolph, who survived him, and another daughter, Maria Eppes, who died before him.

As we ascended the mountain, we noticed the remains of several roads which wound around the hill. These were made by Jefferson for exercise on horseback, but being out of use now, they are partly overgrown with shrubbery. Passing through another rustic gate near the top of the hill we came out into an open field on the southern summit, along the slope of which stretches, for a thousand feet, a beautiful terraced garden, once filled with the choicest plants, and fruit trees. A few moments afterward, we were standing upon the eastern front of the venerated mansion. . . .

Alas! [Wirt's] charming picture of the interior of Monticello is *only a picture now*—it has no counterpart in reality. Those Indian relics, the scultures and paintings, the fossils and minerals, have long since been removed and scattered; and nothing now remains at Monticello of all that fine collection, but a bust of Voltaire. The beauty and grandeur of the aspect of nature around are undiminished; and never did my heart beat with stronger pulsations of delight in gazing upon a prospect of the material world, than on that sunny afternoon in March, although the hills and valleys were clad in the melancholy russet and sober gray of departing winter. Yet there remained the lofty summits of the Blue Ridge, leading the eye away northward, almost a hundred miles to Harper's Ferry, where the Potomac bursts through; and in the rolling valley in that direction reposed the pretty village of Charlottesville, with its fine architectural pile—a monument of Jefferson's taste and patriotism—the University of Virginia. A little further westward is Lewis's mountain, upon a spur of which is the observatory of the University; and half a mile eastward of the village, between it and the Rivanna, near a grove of pines, was depicted in delicate green, the meadow where Tarleton was encamped an hour before sending a detachment up the Rivanna to seize the Governor. Four or five miles beyond, toward the Blue Ridge, arose Still-house Mountain, a wooded eminence where the captive troops of Burgoyne were encamped for many months. Three miles eastward of Monticello, among the hills of Shadwell, is the birth place of Jefferson; and upon the Rivanna, which courses along the base of Monticello, and is lost to view among the adjacent hills, is the old Shadwell mill. Turning southward, Willis's Mountain, a solitary peak in Buckingham county, beyond the James River, fifty miles distant, arose above the level country around. An extensive view in every direction is broken only by the higher summit of Carter's mountain, half a mile southwestward, which rather appreciates than diminishes the charm of the whole picture. In the same range of hills, ten miles northward, is *Montpelier,* the residence of President Madison; and three or four miles southward is *Indian Camp,* once an estate of President Monroe.

Monticello is now owned by Commodore U. P. Levy, of the United States Navy, who is also the proprietor of Monroe's estate. His winter residence is in the city of New York. Fortunately for me, he arrived at Monticello on the day of my visit, and I had the pleasure of viewing the house and grounds while partaking of his hospitality. The elements have changed the aspect of the exterior somewhat, but in general appearance it is the same as when Jefferson left it. The interior, likewise, remains unchanged, except in furniture and other movables. In the "spacious and lofty hall" only one object of the sculptor's art remains. It is a model, in plaster, of the capital, composed by Mr. Jefferson[2] for a new order of architecture, purely American, in which the column was to consist of a group of maize or Indian corn stalks. The capital has the same general form and style as the Corinthian, but the ornaments are composed of the leaves and blossoms of the tobacco plant, regularly grouped, instead of the acanthus.

Near the capital, upon a pedestal, stood a bust of Jefferson in plaster, made in the same mould in which was cast the fine, life-size, bronze statue of the Patriot, which now stands in front of the executive mansion at Washington.[3] That statue is from the *atelier* of the celebrated David, of Paris. It was made for Captain Levy, at a heavy cost, and presented by him to the United States about twenty years ago. It was modeled chiefly from an excellent portrait of Jefferson by Sully, in the possession of La Fayette, and passed the ordeal of that venerated patriot's criticism. When completed, he pronounced it a most faithful counterfeit of the man. Upon the scroll, held in the hand of the Patriot, the whole of the Declaration of Independence is engraved.

Near the bust of Jefferson stood a beautiful model of the *Vandalia*, the first ship in our Navy in which flogging was abolished, while she was under the command of Captain Levy. Upon the wall, close by, is a fine portrait of Madame Noel (an aunt of Captain Levy, and also of the late Major Noah, the veteran New York editor) wife of M. Noel, a member of the National Assembly of France, who was guillotined during the Reign of Terror. She was afterward a tutor of the Princess Charlotte of England, in a peculiar style of flower painting. The portrait was painted by Sir Joshua Reynolds. Two or three more modern paintings adorn the walls of the hall. Over the entrance door from the portico, is a large clock, placed there by Jefferson, which, by an index upon the wall, indicated the days of the week. The weight which propels it is composed of nine eighteen pound cannon balls. The hall itself is about thirty feet square, with high ceiling and a music gallery. The centre of the ceiling is ornamented by an eagle in very low relief, surrounded by eighteen stars, the number of the State in the Union in 1812, when this ceiling was made. The heavy, richly-wrought cornice, carved in wood, in this and the other rooms, all exhibit a line of ornament at the base, representing ancient sacrificial implements.

Adjoining the hall, is the saloon where Jefferson entertained his visitors. It is a superb room, about the size of the hall, with a very high ceiling, and a beautiful tesselated floor, made of inlaid satin-wood and rose-wood. This floor, which was kept polished like a table, cost two thousand dollars. Of all the rare pictures and other ornaments which once adorned the walls, nothing now remains but two mirrors, four and a half by twelve feet in size. They hang, one upon each side of the door opening into the hall. Over the door is the gilt bracket or crane, upon which hung the chandelier that lighted the room.

On the southeast side of the hall and saloon is Jefferson's bedroom, which was also his most private apartment for study, and contemplation. It is lighted by two windows on the southwest, and a skylight. The bedstead was only a frame, hung upon hinges and hooks in the recess, seen in the centre. It could be turned up in the day time, and afford a passage through glass doors, to his library in the adjoining room.[4] The three oval openings in the wall were for the purpose of admitting light to a wardrobe over the recess.

On the northwest side of the hall and saloon is the tea-room, which contains a most delicately carved white marble chimney-piece ornamented with three exquisite *basso relievos,* upon a sky-blue ground. Adjoining this apartment is one in which he held private conference with his friends. It is separated from the tea-room by double glass doors, so that, while the party in secret communication could be seen by guests in the other room, not a word could be heard. In this room was the bust of Voltaire, alluded to. The sashes of the glass doors, like those of all the windows in the house, are of mahogany, and were made in Philadelphia.

The stairs are all winding and very narrow, not more than two feet wide. On the northeast part of the second floor is a chamber of hexagonal form, wherein Mr. and Mrs. Madison were lodged whenever they visited Monticello. Except his own immediate family, these were the dearest friends of Mr. Jefferson. From this floor another flight of stairs lead to the upper chambers, adjoining which is a spacious hexagonal room under the dome, lighted by circular windows on the sides. This was used for a billiard-room. In it was an interesting memento of the statesman. It was the body of the *chair* or *gig,* a two wheeled vehicle, in which Jefferson rode from Monticello to Philadelphia, to attend the Continental Congress in 1775. Near this hung his holsters, in which he carried a pair of pistols when traveling on horseback.

The shade trees which form an open grove around the mansion were planted by the Patriot himself. Among them, standing near the southern end of the building, is a venerable Lombardy poplar ... which he imported from its native soil in Europe. From this have sprung all the trees of that species in this country. It has flourished there for about sixty years, and unlike many of its descendants, appears to retain the vigor of its youth. . . .

Benson J. Lossing, "Monticello," *Harper's New Monthly Magazine* 7 (1853): 145–51.

1. Castle Hill.

2. A frequent error; the design was Latrobe's.

3. Buckingham, on the other hand, said he saw the "full-length statue."

4. This account is perhaps the source of a persistent myth about the bed.

◅ 1 8 6 2 ▻

Johnny Reb
at Monticello

NO GREAT CIVIL WAR BATTLES occurred in Jefferson's country. Yet it was in the path of marching armies, both Union and
Confederate, and Monticello was sometimes visited en route.
What follows is a distant recollection of a common soldier,
B. L. Aycock, in General John B. Hood's Texas Brigade. He
had peculiar ideas about bees and Jefferson and the English
equivalent of Monticello, but his recollection of the events
leading up to the Seven Days' Battle and General McClellan's
withdrawal from Richmond was accurate.

IT WAS JUNE OF 1862, and on the eleventh orders came to get out of
the Chickahominy Swamp to move on to Richmond to take the cars
(box cars)—entrained for where? It was General Lee's first strategic
movement. General Johnston had been disabled at Seven Pines (Fair
Oaks, as this battle was called by the Yankees). This was the first
station on the York River Railroad out of Richmond. All aboard and
headed, as it looked to a private soldier, for Lynchburg, thence to
Charlottesville, where we spent a Sunday and went to church; seats
occupied by women and children, men conspicuous by their absence.
What the preacher's text was I can't recall, but he dwelt upon the sore
treatment of Christ the Lord.

Monday or Tuesday orders came to move five miles to the Fluvanna
River,¹ which we crossed on a bridge, entering a long lane, a gentle
slope from Monticello to the little stream, the boundary of the farm
once the pride of the famous statesman, Thomas Jefferson. At the top,
the front gate of the grounds seemed to irresistibly invite, "Come in,"

144

so some of us went in without "unlatching" our shoes and stood on the front porch of Monticello. Did we stand on sacred portals? The name translated is "Honey Mount." We did not see the bees at work at the rear of the house, which reminds that the statesman could handle them without being stung; bees know their friends. Thomas Jefferson evidently found the name *Monticello*. What glorious memories cluster around it, and there his thoughts crystalized into the immortal Declaration of Independence. Democracy—or, "we the people, by the people, and for the people." Rule free from the domination of foreign potentates, rulers, and princes.

On from here we went a few hour's march to the Rock Bridge, on and on a leisurely march till we, as Lee's dependables, were marching facing Richmond from Gordonsville. On this stretch another Sunday. Stonewall had joined us, and he held services in his tent. Ah, this was company indeed!

A few more days and the guns of A. P. Hill were the signal. He had struck at Mechanicsville, where the Seven Days' Battles began; and he put Fitzjohn Porter to his wit's end and "Little Mack" lifted the siege of the Confederate capital. But O! that day, the 27th of June, the attack at Gaines's Mill, the bloody struggle it was! Fourteen Federal guns were the trophy of Hood's Texas Brigade. Night gave Porter its cover to get away. The siege of Richmond was raised.

B. L. Aycock, "Monticello," *Confederate Veteran* 34 (1926): 7. Reprinted by permission.

1. The river was the Rivanna.

⚜ 1872 ⚜

⁊

A Student's
Excursion

FROM THE TIME THE University of Virginia opened in 1825, students have been going to Monticello. David M. R. Culbreath entered the university in the fall of 1872, and on the first bright Sunday he and a friend set forth on foot for Jefferson's mountain. Culbreath, too, dwelled on the melancholy spectacle of the tomb. Interestingly, he conjectured that relic hunters had taken the marble slab from the monument; but some thirty years earlier Buckingham observed it affixed to a wall in the house. Culbreath saw Monticello in its most dilapidated state. The account, which is full of curious information, was written from diary notes some thirty-five years later and published in the author's book, *The University of Virginia*.

BURRUS AND I started for Monticello at 11.30 o'ck.; stopped at Ambroselli's for oysters and waffles, knowing we would miss regular dinner; left restaurant an hour later and journeyed the usual route to Charlottesville, thence out by the depot, the only one in those days over the railroad tracks by the private road, on the crest, through Mr. Ficklin's two farms, thence up hill and down dale to intersect the regular winding road around the base and in the notch between the higher Carter's Mountain on the south and Monticello, reaching the latter's summit by a tortuous road over its southwestern slope. Our pace was rather rapid until nearing the mountain's base we encountered and unexpected obstacle—a good-sized stream without bridge or foot-log. This vehicles easily forded, but none of these was in sight, nor likely to be on the holy day—a time not justifying much passing to and from town. While deliberating our troubles two students joined us having in common the same destination, so we four proceeded up the stream until a point was reached with many bed-rocks protruding above the running water and sufficiently close together to be reached by forced effort in jumping. This enabled our safe passage and the entrance shortly thereafter upon the ascent of the mountain side covered densely with a growth of small and larger trees. Hill climbing at best requires the expenditure of much energy—means work—but to pull one's self up that narrow, poorly made and kept rocky, precipitious road, taking cross-cuts whenever possible, suggested early the nature of our impending task and the wish that the summit be less remote. After tugging quite an hour we came upon the graveyard, laying near to and on the right (east) of the road, an area of more than a hundred feet square enclosed by a brick wall of at least eight feet high. An iron gate slightly higher than the wall and about ten feet wide, constructed of three horizontal and many vertical rods four inches apart, guarded the entrance on the roadside (northwest), which was locked securely. We stood a while gazing through these wide meshes, and except in the immediate front the view was that of a neglected wilderness—thoroughly covered with an undergrowth of grass, small and large bushes and a few stately trees. In the foreground several feet from the gate and about its median line stood a modest monument, obelisk, eight feet high, with square base three feet broad and two feet high, surmounted by a tapering rectangular shaft with base two feet and apex ten to twelve inches, the latter beveled on all four sides to form an obtuse point. To our left could easily be seen several graves covered with full-sized horizontal marble and slate slabs, and in the rear wall one or two disintegrated crumbling spots, by which we concluded an entrance might be effected without risk or injury—a surmise well-founded as in a few minutes we faced the lettered side (east) of the monument. On the granite base could partly be made out in three lines:

Born April 2d.
1743, O. S.
Died July 4th, 1826.

In the main shaft above was an indentation, into which was fastened originally a white marble plate or slab bearing the following inscription—that which Mr. Jefferson during life purposely wrote and placed

Monticello in ruin: east front. Photograph by William Roads, about 1870.
(*Prints File, Manuscripts Division, Special Collections Department,
University of Virginia Library.*)

The tomb of Jefferson. Photograph, about 1871.
(*Hitchcock Family Photographs (acc. no. 9822-f), Manuscripts Division,
Special Collections Department, University of Virginia Library.*)

Visitors in the 1870s. Photograph.
(*Courtesy of the Thomas Jefferson Memorial Foundation, Inc.*)

in a certain private drawer along with various souvenirs, including and ink sketch of the monument he desired:

Here was buried
THOMAS JEFFERSON
Author of the Declaration of American Independence,
Of the Statute of Virginia for Religious Freedom,
And Father of the University of Virginia.

There was not a vestige left of this inlaid slab, but it must have conformed in outline to the the full tapering face of the shaft, nearly two feet wide, and have been that high, as the visible recession extended from within three inches of the base to the shaft's median line. Of course the marble slab, soft compared with the rest of the monument, had been broken and chipped off by the relic hunters, whose ruthless hands ceased not even there, but had made disfiguring inroads upon all four of the square corner, these being irregularly broken their entire length. Seeing what others had done—set a vulgar example— encouraged me to possess a similar memento of my visit, so with various pieces of rocks lying around I attempted to break off small fragments, but in vain as the harder granite sternly resisted the violence applied. I did, however, find within twenty feet of the grave a straight growing scion, which I cut, had ferruled and capped, to serve me many years as a curious walking stick. Although Mr. Jefferson lay buried between his wife and daughter, Mary, with his eldest daughter, Martha, across the head, all having had appropriate marble slabs, yet only a few fragments of Martha's, the longest survivor, remained to tell the story. . . .

After carefully inspecting everything considered of interest we re-scaled the rear wall and continued our steps to the slightly more elevated summit, not more than a fourth of a mile distant, which we found practically level for a space of six hundred feet north and south by three hundred east and west, to serve as a lawn, the sides of the mountain gradually sloping therefrom. Stately trees stood here and there, and near the center the neglected mansion, facing north—more accurately northeast—to whose approach a straight indented but thoroughly overgrown walk led from the lawn's edge. It seemed closed and unoccupied, but upon walking around to various points of advantage, talking considerably, and showing signs of curiosity, an elderly white man made his appearance. He was the keeper living on the premises (several south rooms), having the privilege of certain tillage and the revenue from showing visitors through the house—that for us being the modest sum of fifteen cents each. In this capacity he had acted for years, knew considerable Jeffersonian history, and delighted to communicate it. The mountain had a height of about six hundred feet and contains two hundred and twenty-three acres, only one-half being subject to cultivation. The building, externally Doric, internally Ionic architecture, is constructed of English bricks, much discolored, apparently a single story with balustrade around the almost flat roof cornice, and consists of one large octagonal pavilion surmounted by a circular dome, having wings north and south, and projecting porticoes east and west—each cross-section being about one hundred feet. The north and south wings each terminate in a piazza with same floor elevation as the house, three feet, supported by brick arches, and opening on to a terrace, one-third above and two-thirds under ground—whose floors are of the same level as the cellar with which they communicate, and whose nearly flat roofs are on a line with the first floor, thus enabling their use for promenading in evenings and damp weather. These terraces extend to the brow of the mountain on either side, having their two projecting ends terminating in additional storied turrets or pavilions, twenty feet square, both having been used by Mr. Jefferson as offices—the south one in winter, the north one in summer—where he was accustomed to sit bareheaded until bedtime with friends, unannoyed by dew and insects. The north one was occupied many years as an office by his grandson, Thomas Jefferson Randolph,[1] and it was through one of these, possibly the southern, that Mr. Jefferson, when Governor, made escape, thus evading capture by the British under Tarleton. The mansion contains thirty-six rooms, small and large, and has two almost similar entrances—east and west—the former considered front, having a portico receding six feet within the wall, thereby giving it depth of twenty-five and a width of thirty feet, covered by an angled roof supported by four stout stone pillars resting on the floor, three feet above ground, and reached by five or six low stone steps extending its entire width. It was through this our guide admitted us, entering first a lofty nearly square hall or saloon having balcony to the right, connecting the upper story and originally intended an avenue of reaching the first floor by ornamental stairways—those that never were erected. On one side is an old bust of Mr. Jefferson and opposite stands one of Hamilton, both mounted on large pedestals; over the front door built into the wall is a good sized clock, which had to be wound standing upon a ladder—this latter being in normal position and claimed to have been made by Mr. Jefferson himself; the hands stand at 7.34 o'ck. From this hall we passed through folding glass doors into an octagonal parlor or drawing-room, twenty-six by twenty-three feet, opening out upon the rear or west portico, so that these two large rooms comprise the entire depth of the house. The parlor is adorned with several pictures, and French plate mirrors extending from ceiling to floor, the latter being tessellated or parqueted in ten inch squares of wild cherry (mahogany color) with four inch borders of light-colored beech, finished with a glossy surface. From these two large halls or rooms we entered the other living apartments—from the east hall by a passage on the right to two bedrooms and the piazza, by one on the left (south) to Mrs. Jefferson's[2] sitting-room, library and piazza; from the west hall (parlor) we entered on the right (north) a good-sized dining-room furnished with a handsome crystal chandelier and busts of Washington, Lafayette and Voltaire, while just beyond (northward) is an octagonal tea-room, used alone by Mr. Jefferson, opening out upon the north piazza; from the parlor on the left (south) was Mr. Jefferson's room which entered, as did the adjoining passage, into the library—a room extending the full depth of the building and opening by glass windows and doors upon the piazza enclosed with glass for a conservatory. The upper story, reached by a very narrow, dark, winding stairs admitting the passage of only one person at a time, is divided into a number of small irregular shaped, poorly lighted and ventilated rooms, several having alcoves with slats fastened into them for beds, like unto the bed-chambers on the lower floor. The dome room is octagonal, large and commodious, without any partitions, being used in its palmy day as the "ladies' drawing room," but now the repository of one solitary article of more than passing interest—the sulky or gig body in which Mr. Jefferson made frequent trips to Richmond, Washington, Philadelphia, etc. In one of the upper bedrooms a member of the family died, when it was found necessary to lower the body through one of the front circular windows, the stairs being too contracted for that purpose. Upon approaching by the front entrance the octagon with its circular dome is scarcely visible, as that occupies the rear half of the building, but looms into conspicuous prominence and effect when one approaches from the graveyard or rear.

Monticello of that day was a total wreck, as many years had passed without the slightest effort at repairs; the shingles of the roof were so decayed as not only to admit rain and snow but the rays of sunlight; many window panes, slats and shutters were broken or missing; the paint of former years was scarcely visible, and everything, once bright and beautiful was stained and effaced. The old English bricks, as durable as time, were darkened by exposure, while the covered ways (terraces) were coated with mould and green deposit, the result of dampness, darkness and neglect. The front was carved, penciled and disfigured with the names and remarks of many who could not omit registering the delightful occasion of the visitation.

That day's experience at Monticello was attended with no little sadness, indeed, depression, for everything observed belonged to a passed generation, had apparently seen its day of usefulness and was on the rapid road to extinction. No one, seemingly, was left with sufficient means, interest or patriotism to stay the inroad of decay, and the entire mountain top stood in our minds hopelessly doomed. One could scarcely realize the historic side of the place, especially the facts: that there possibly above all other private spots in America had been assembled most love of liberty, virtue, wisdom and learning; that it had been the home of Mr. Jefferson for sixty years, forty of which, having been spent in higher positions of public trust, had occasioned a certain degree of entertaining unsurpassed in its day; that Madison, Monroe, Wirt, Henry, Randolph and others had used so frequently its hospitality as their own, while Webster, Paine, Priestley, Ticknor, Wayland, Lafayette and hundreds of more or less eminence had wandered around those grounds as were we that beautiful afternoon of perfect sunshine. Although this was my maiden trip to the "bleak house on the hill top," yet no year passed during my stay at the University without making at least one visit to that sacred shrine. It was the custom of quite a number of us students and many fair daughters of Albemarle to unite in giving upon those spacious and secluded grounds annual May-parties, and the days thus spent stand out now in after life with unusual brightness. Each year we found it the same dilapidated, heartrending object, experiencing no change save for the worse, presided over by the old keeper, more dead than alive, ever glad to greet a strange and youthful face, and when in numbers, as on those festive May occasions, his joy knew no bounds, for we not only brought him abundant sunshine, but what possibly was more appreciated and to his liking—many dainties and dimes. No one enjoyed more than he the coronation of the May Queen and the reverberations through that grove and palatial mansion of music's sweet strains furnished by the Charlottesville String Bang.

David M. R. Culbreath, *The University of Virginia* (Washington, D.C., 1908), 217–23.

1. It is best remembered as the office of Jefferson's son-in-law Thomas Mann Randolph.

2. Mrs. Randolph presumably is meant.

A Tour of Jefferson M. Levy's Monticello

AT THE TURN OF THE CENTURY Monticello was coming prom-
inently into public view. A writer for popular magazines,
Maud Howard Peterson, offers a glimpse of the house during
Jefferson M. Levy's occupancy. She approved of his trustee-
ship and understated the extent of his innovations. Some of
these, like the billiard table in the dome room, contributed to
the strains of legend and error in her account. The story she
tells of John Marshall is apocryphal; nor was any law ban-
ning billiards passed in Virginia, nor did Jefferson intend the
dome room for billiards, nor was it converted into a ballroom. Peterson's article, with many illustrations, appeared in
Munsey's Magazine in 1899.

"VIRGINIA?" said a loyal son of the Old Dominion—and all sons of
the Old Dominion are loyal ones. "Oh, yes, all the other States, you
know, are surrounded with mountains and water and other States, but
Virginia is surrounded with a halo!"

Certainly no American commonwealth has a greater wealth of romantic memories and historical associations. From the time of John
Smith and Pocahontas down to the Civil War and after, Virginia, with
her forest clad hills and broad valleys, had done her share, and more,
in the making of our history. . . .

No name in her record stands for more of Virginia's good and glory
than that of Thomas Jefferson. Steadily, desperately, he fought for her
religious freedom, and for the independence of his country; and he
raised his own memorial when he planned and built the university of

Jefferson M. Levy's Monticello: east front. Photograph, about 189
(Holsinger Studio Collection (acc. no. 9862), Manuscripts Divisio

variously attributed to R. W. Holsinger and to Rhodes & Carter.
Special Collections Department, University of Virginia Library.)

Entrance hall. Photograph by R. W. Holsinger,
Manuscripts Division, Special Collections

912. (*Holsinger Studio Collection (acc. no. 9862),*
)epartment, University of Virginia Library.)

546

Entrance hall. Photograph by R. W. Holsinger.
Manuscripts Division, Special Collections

1912. (*Holsinger Studio Collection (acc. no. 9862),*
Department, University of Virginia Library.)

Dining room. Photograph by R. W. Holsinger, about
Manuscripts Division, Special Collections

1912. (*Holsinger Studio Collection (acc. no. 9862),*
Department, University of Virginia Library.)

his State. Of his public career, of his success in foreign courts, of his ability as a diplomat, of his steering of the ship of state as our third President, long histories have been written. It is strange, therefore, that that which he held most closely to his heart—his life at Monticello, and the years spent in planning the university—have been so little touched on.

Three miles from Shadwell, his birthplace; four from the town of Charlottesville, and six from where the great rotunda shows above the trees, and the arcades planned by him stretch out long shadows over the broad lawn, Jefferson built his home. It stands on the summit of a hill, commanding one of the finest views in all the county of Albemarle, and bearing the name he gave it, Monticello, meaning "little mountain."

The approach is steep. Half a mile from the house is a lodge, erected a few years ago by the present owner, where an old time "uncle" greets you and opens wide the gates. The driveway runs through a grove of trees. Further on one passes through another gateway, and, between low hedges of osage orange bushes, reaches the curving entrance to the house itself. The building stands on the highest point of ground, with its great red bricks, massive white pillars, and low French windows of square paned glass, forming a crown of glory to the "little mountain."

While time and friendly care have dealt kindly with the fine old home, in a few details it has changed since Jefferson's day. What he used to term the "front lawn" is now considered the rear. Indeed, there is some question just which Jefferson himself regarded as the entrance. The body of the house begun in 1765 and finished in 1773, was doubtless added to some years later, and the appearance of the west lawn was changed. Off the south, near to the house, stand the original quarters of the servants, a long row of low brick building with white trimmings. Near to them, separated only by the carriage road, one can see the little white house, with its red brown roof and green blinds, that was the home of Jefferson's overseer.

The interior of Monticello is as quaint as it is beautiful. The principal architectual feature is the hall in the center of the house, thirty feet square, with a ceiling extending beyond the second story. Half way around it runs the gallery, with its slender white railing, upon which the bedrooms of the second story open. Directly opposite the entrance to the hall is the salon, the floor of which is inlaid with sat-inwood and rosewood, which, in spite of the passing of the years, is as smooth and level as when put down, more than a century ago. Indeed, all floors and all the woodwork of the house are still as the builder left them—massive, with rich carvings, defying time, and only mellowing and growing more beautiful with the flight of years.

To the left of the salon is Jefferson's bed chamber: a deep archway separating it from his study, which is the extreme end room of the southwest wing of the house. For some strange reason, Jefferson was opposed to beds, and in drawing the plans for Monticello he arranged that in every bed chamber an alcove should be built, across which, from end to end, should be placed slats, and on these, mattresses. In his own particular bedroom he had the alcove constructed as an arch, so that both sides should be open; one entering into his private study, the other to his bed chamber proper. The space above the arch is hol-low; its interior, with small round windows opening into the bed chamber, forms a little room in which his serving man always slept within immediate call. This curious sleeping apartment is reached by passing through a closet door and up a narrow flight of stairs.

From Jefferson's study, walking forward, one enters the library, which can also be reached by a narrow passage extending from the main hall. Opposite the great man's bedroom is the chamber once occupied by his married daughter, Mrs. Randolph. In the right wing, corresponding to Mrs. Randolph's room and part of the library, are two bed chambers, which, tradition tells us, were at one time and another occupied by Madison, Monroe, and the Abbé Correa de Serra, the Portuguese savant and diplomat. Directly above, on the second story, are rooms in which Lafayette and Adams are said to have slept when they visited Monticello.

Connecting with the salon on the right is the diningroom, and still beyond, the beautiful little tea room in which Jefferson sat in the after-noons, and from which he would step out of the low French window, with its quaint square panes, to the terrace below.

On the third floor is the famous ballroom, built originally for bil-liards of which Jefferson was extremely fond. Scarcely was it com-pleted, however, when he discovered, to his chagrin, that the game was prohibited by a law recently passed by the State Legislature. The story runs that some years earlier there lived within the borders of

Virginia a very brilliant and promising young lawyer named John Marshall, who insisted on wasting his time on games of all sorts, and most especially on billiards. In vain his friends urged him to work seriously and give up such unprofitable pastimes. Marshall was not to be moved. Finally some one suggested that a law should be enacted to suppress billiards, declaring that "Marshall would never break a law." The State Legislature, at the time, was composed largely of the young man's friends, and they passed the necessary bill. They laughingly used to say, afterwards, that Marshall owed to their timely intervention his subsequent brilliant career, which made him chief justice of the United States Supreme Court.

However, the fact remains that billiards were prohibited throughout Virginia; and Jefferson, with the calm philosophy that characterized so much of his life, made the best of a bad bargain, and the room was converted into a ballroom, perhaps the most famous in any private residence of the time. Could its walls speak, they would tell strange tales of the beauty, gallantry, and wit that once assembled there. It was to have been approached by stairways connected with a gallery at the inner extremity of the hall. For some unknown reason these were never erected; instead, a staircase was built in each wing, of such narrow dimensions that it is still a problem how the grand ladies with their ample hoopskirts ever ascended to the ballroom above.

The rustle of their silk brocades has ceased; the soft music of Mrs. Randolph's harpsichord has melted into space; the powdered heads, the ruffles and knee breeches, are no longer to be seen; but in spite of the changes that have come with the years, about the old place still lingers something of the spirit of Jefferson.

In the ceiling of the lofty portico is the round faced weather vane with its long slender hands, planned by him. One can still see the impress of the horse's hoof in the hall, where a British soldier rode when he came to capture the fiery patriot. One can still see the famous clock high above the entrance door, double faced, with its great weights of Revolutionary cannon balls, designed by Jefferson to mark not only the time of day but the day of the week as well—the great clock with its gong to mark the hours, the strokes of which can be heard six miles away at the university, to remind its students of their founder. One can still see the folding ladder he invented to reach the clock, and the great iron key with which it is wound; and in the sides of the diningroom mantel are still the little doors, which open and reveal two small dumbwaiters, just large enough to hold bottles of wine, connecting directly with the wine cellar beneath.

Long ago, when Jefferson lived, the great kitchen, after the Southern fashion, was situated away from the house, near to the servants' quarters. At meal time negro boys were stationed along the path that led from it to the mansion, and dish after dish was swiftly passed down the line until it reached the butler in the diningroom. So skillful were the boys that rarely a plate was broken, and the food was still hot when it reached the family. This kitchen has since been burned.

Jefferson was peculiarly kind to his servants—real Southerners never spoke of them as slaves—and on more than one occasion took the place of physician as well as friend. . . .

Too much credit cannot be given Mr. Levy for his intelligent care of the home and grounds. While ample means have restored much of their original beauty, no modern innovation has come in. It is his policy and his pride to keep the old house, the green terraces, the wide lawns, and the ancient trees as they were in the hands of their first owner. From time to time, whenever possible, he has bought back an original bit of statuary or furniture—a difficult task, when one remembers how widely scattered such things were after Jefferson's death, and later by confiscation. True, the great trees are larger than when Jefferson stood beneath their shade with his spyglass to watch the building of the University, and if not satisfied rode down to make things right. Within the last year another road has been cut through the deep woods leading out of the place, as the original one (which is still used as the approach) was too narrow for carriages to pass safely when coming in opposite directions. Some time ago visitors to the place became so numerous and so destructive that Mr. Levy established a moderate fee for entrance to the grounds, the proceeds being made over to the hospital in Charlottesville. Of late, however, this has been done away with, and only persons bearing a permit signed by the owner are allowed to enter. Visitors average from twenty five to seventy five a day, and truth compels the statement that many have taken advantage of Mr. Levy's kindness and have pulled flowers, barked trees, and otherwise disfigured the place in the effort to carry away souvenirs. Indeed, one relic hunter was so lost to all the debt of courtesy that he (or she) picked out from the mantel in the dining-room, during the family's absence, the rare old Wedgwood plaques presented to Jefferson by the maker himself. Copies, which Mr. Levy immediately had made, now take the place of the originals.

Half way up between the lodge gates and the house, a little back from the carriage house, and overshadowed by tall trees, is the one spot on the estate that is still owned by Jefferson's descendents. It is the burying ground; and here Jefferson and generations of his kin profoundly sleep. . . .

Maud Howard Peterson, "The Home of Jefferson," *Munsey's Magazine* 20 (1899): 609–18.

⌡

A Democratic Pilgrimage
to Monticello

THOMAS JEFFERSON was the patron saint of the Democratic party. Nowhere, outside of Virginia, was his memory as green as in Missouri. In 1901 the Jefferson Club of St. Louis, which called itself "the most consistently Jeffersonian association" in the country, was virtually identical with the city's ruling Democratic party. Seeking to dramatize its ties to Jefferson's name and principles, the club made a 900-mile pilgrimage to Monticello and there dedicated a granite monument to the author of the Louisiana Purchase. The record of these events is preserved in a book, *The Pilgrimage to Monticello by the Jefferson Club of St. Louis.*

WHEN . . . AT A MEETING OF THE CLUB, on August 1st, 1901, the President, Mr. Harry B. Hawes, offered resolutions calling for committee action that would specifically and significantly signalize devotion to the principles of Jefferson at a time when there were just fears that the Republic was drifting away from the doctrines of human rights held by Jefferson, there was a spontaneous adoption of the resolutions by acclamation. The resolutions themselves, expressing fully the purpose of the commemoration, are as follows:

> *Resolved, that this committee, pursuant to the instruction of the Board of Directors, shall perfect arrangements for a trip to Monticello, Va., for the purpose of doing honor to the memory of Thomas Jefferson; that all those persons who believe in the principles and teachings of Thomas Jefferson shall*

be eligible for invitation to join in the pilgrimage of the club members.

Resolved, further, that the trip shall be taken on Thursday night, October 10th, 1901, leaving St. Louis at that time and returning the following Monday morning, October 14th, 1901. That each person attending shall pay the sum of $25.00, which will include transportation, sleeping car fare and meals both ways, and that the balance of the expense of the trip shall be borne by the Jefferson Club or by voluntary subscription.

Be it further Resolved, that the Jefferson Club shall take with it a rough block of Missouri granite with one polished surface, upon which a suitable inscription shall be made commemorating the pilgrimage. That this block shall be so arranged that a receptacle shall be provided for the deposit of a parchment roll containing the names of all those persons who take part in the pilgrimage.

Forthwith the preparations for the pilgrimage were begun with energy. Committees were appointed to attend to every detail and in due course the completion of the arrangements was announced and on Thursday evening, October 10, 1901, a train of six coaches left the Union Station in St. Louis bearing to Monticello the members of the Jefferson Club and invited guests, numbering in all more than two hundred and fifty. The ride was rendered delightful by the balmy weather, by the panorama of beautiful scenery amid which the excursion wound its way through half a dozen great States, and by the comradery of the party. Arriving in Charlottesville, Va., about midnight of October 11th, and resting until Saturday morning, the 12th, the large party, preceded by a band, with the National colors flying, were conveyed in vehicles furnished by the citizens of Charlottesville to Monticello, the home and tomb of Jefferson.

Needless to say that the gathering was impressed by the sublimity of the scene as its members looked away from Jefferson's mountain through the disappearing mists of the morning, across valleys of rolling farm land to other mountains, or that each one experienced an even deeper feeling as he thought that he was standing on the ground rendered forever sacred by the life and deeds, the death and dust of one who had been the greatest benefactor of mankind. The stately home he had reared impressed by its dignity and strength and grace of outline. The trees that sheltered the pilgrims from a heavy dew, Jefferson himself had planted. Here he had walked, resolving the puzzles of government, or had stood gazing out over the peaceful valleys and absorbing the serenity of the scene before him, widening his mind almost unconsciously by observing the majestic sweep of the lands below and taking to himself the strength of the eternal hills about him. The pilgrims stood by his tomb and felt how well it became the man in its simplicity. They caught from the surroundings something of the flavor of the character that had developed amid the beautiful and strong environment.

Famed Monticello was thrown open to the visitors by the present occupant, Hon. Jefferson M. Levy, who holds it, as he says, as trustee for the people Jefferson loved. Through the historic mansion the visitors roamed at will, inspecting its art treasures, entering the rooms in which Jefferson lived his daily life for long years, familiarizing themselves with the things with which Jefferson's eyes and hands had been familiar while his greatest work was being done. Mr. Levy and the ladies of his household graciously received the visitors and by their courteous guidance and explanations made additionally interesting the visit to the scenes of the most intimate incidents of the life of a great friend of man. The house speaks eloquently of the man who built it. It has the quiet dignity in ease, the evidence of artistic feeling, the intimation of open-mindedness and open-heartedness, the suggestion of culture that one draws from a study of Jefferson's writings and character. The house is the expression of the man who built it and lived in it, and it stands out on the hill with much of the same sort of grace and calm and strength with which Jefferson himself stands out among the great men of the country upon which he, more than any other of his time, with the possible exception of Washington, left the impress of his mighty individuality. The scene, the air of the place, the memories aroused, the patriotic emotions vivified by the associations, the inrushing sense of the full meaning of Jefferson in the history of the modern world of thought and action, all these made for a sentiment of tenderness for the man who died there only to live forever in a Nation's life, and the pilgrims felt indeed, according to their capacities for feeling, that they had not in vain traveled nearly a thousand miles when they caught the thrill and glow of a mental and moral and spiritual uplift, standing at the shrine of one who loved, if ever man did, his fellow men.

The reception of the pilgrimage by the ladies of the household having concluded, and the pilgrims having inscribed their names in the visitors' book of the historic mansion, the assemblage gathered on the lawn before the house and there were welcomed to Monticello by Hon. Jefferson M. Levy. Mr. Levy spoke as follows:

Ladies and Members of the Jefferson Club of St. Louis, Citizens of Missouri and Virginia:

I welcome you to the home of Thomas Jefferson. Your visit honors the memory of the greatest statesman and profoundest thinker of any time or country.

All people who love free and unrestricted liberty and the ideal principles of republican government, now recognize Jefferson as the father of true Democracy. His principles apply to-day to the government of seventy-five millions of people as they applied in our early history to a few people.

While, citizens of Missouri, he secured your country through his diplomacy, he also secured to the Middle West from the Virginia Commonwealth, the concession of the Northwestern Reserve which now contains the great States of Ohio, Indiana, Illinois, Michigan, Wisconsin and Minnesota.

Turn to any question of government, finance, dealings with foreign powers, acquisition of territory, commerce, education, coinage—in fact, to every public subject before the people now, or in the past, and you will find his principles applicable, and tending to lead our country to become the greatest nation in the world. Our late beloved and patriotic President, William McKinley, whose death our people are now lamenting, stated to me a short time before his death, that each day of his life he learned more and more of Jefferson, that he never tired of reading his writings, and that in the administration of his office as President, he ever sought to put his principles into practice.

Therefore, fellow citizens, it gives me great pleasure to greet you at his home. You will find it as he left it seventy-five years ago.

I hope all citizens of our country will continue to visit Monticello, for I am sure it cannot but help to inspire our people with a love for our republican form of government. I am sure pilgrimages of this character cannot fail to inspire and unite our party; for as attention is called to the platform of true Democracy, as laid down by Thomas Jefferson, the people will rally round our banners and restore the government to our administration, for it is the only sheet anchor of prosperity.

The Pilgrimage to Monticello by the Jefferson Club of St. Louis (St. Louis, 1902), 5–7.

~⧏ 1902 ⧐~

⟩

A National
Humiliation

IN AN ARTICLE titled "A National Humiliation" Amos J. Cummings, a New York newspaperman, formerly a Democratic congressman, sought in 1902 to draw attention to the plight of Monticello in private hands. Unlike Maud Peterson, he did not consider Jefferson M. Levy a worthy trustee. Cummings's visit to the place actually occurred thirteen years earlier, when he was in Congress. The article was written for the *New York Sun* and afterwards was published as a pamphlet. It is sprightly, amusing, and here and there fanciful.

WASHINGTON, AUG. 24.—The Virginia Midland Railroad runs through a lovely country. Its rolling plains are covered with fertile fields, fruitful orchards, and shady forests. It has a blue sky and a red soil. Its rivers wend to the sea through a rich acreage of grain and tobacco. It presents a magnificent expanse of mountain and valley. An atmosphere of remarkable purity lends an indescribable charm to its scenery. This charm is enhanced by another of strong historic interest. No spot in the Union awakens memories more sad or more patriotic. They flood the heart of every visitor. While travelling over the railroad he sees the green plains of Manassas and beyond them Thoroughfare-Gap, a famed gate to the Valley of the Shenandoah. He hears the waters of the Rappahannock recounting the losses in the assault at Fredericksburg. The river is hardly crossed before the cosey white houses of Culpepper come into view. Beyond it frowning Cedar Mountain casts its shadow. Next he rattles over the Rapidan. Here Revolutionary memories arise and his sad recollections of Civil War drift away upon the river's muddy bosom. Patriotic reflections take their place.

The dreamy Blue Ridge fills the western horizon as the visitor rolls further southward. One after the other, he passes the homesteads of three renowned American Statesmen. Each idealized an epoch in our history. One wrote the Declaration of Independence, the second held the helm of State during the last war with Great Britain; and the third riveted the nation to what is known as the Monroe Doctrine.

All were Virginians and all Democrats. Each remained eight years in the White House. Each served his country honestly, and all died poor. Their descendants are scattered to the four quarters of the earth, and their estates are in the hands of strangers.

The first of these homesteads is Montpelier, once the residence of James Madison. It lies on the left of the railroad, fronting an avenue cut through the forest. The conductor, a Virginian, points it out with true State pride. You catch simply a glimpse of it as the train rolls by.

The second is found some miles below Montpelier. It is Indian Camp, an estate once owned by James Monroe. It has gone to rack and ruin, and shows little trace of its former glory.

You see the third homestead as you approach Charlottesville. It appears in the foliage at the top of a wooded mountain, three miles from the track. The white pillars of its portico gleam in the sunlight. At that distance they recall Arlington, the old home of Robert E. Lee, as seen from Washington. This is Monticello—or "Montichello," as Virginians pronounce it—the home of Thomas Jefferson. It is the most sacred of the three homesteads, for it holds the dust of not only a true patriot, but of the greatest of all Democrats. American hearts have recently been harrowed by a story of its purchase by Judah Levy, late commodore in the United States navy. The story was sent from the University of Virginia, and was printed in the Hartford Courant, edited by Joseph Hawley, United States Senator from Connecticut. Epitomized briefly, it asserts that efforts were made to hold the estate after Jefferson's death for his favorite daughter, Martha Randolph. About $3,000 were required. The money was raised by patriotic Philadelphians, and intrusted to a young Virginian, a relative of Martha Randolph. He got drunk on the way to Monticello, and arrived a day too late. It is more than intimated that Captain Levy, who was a passenger in the same stage, took advantage of his drunkenness and bought the place. The appalled Virginian besought him to be merciful after his purchase, and asked him what he would take for the homestead. His reply was: "Mein frien', you are a glever feller, but you talk too much. I will take a huntret thousand tollars." It was a story that if true,[1] ought to bring the blush of shame to every American face.

My visit to Monticello was paid on the Sunday after the Johnstown disaster.[2] A party of distinguished congressmen, including Senator Plumb of Kansas, Julius Caesar Burrows of Michigan, and William J. Stone of Kentucky, was detained at Charlottesville by a washout on the Midland Railroad. As there was no prospect of escape for twenty-four hours, a tour of the home of Jefferson was proposed. To general surprise, none of the Congressmen accepted it. Which of the three preferred a game of poker and which an hour at church was not ascertained. The Monticello party included an Englishman, a Jersey-man, and an Alabamian. The latter had graduated from the University of Virginia and was upon familiar ground.

Three dollars secure a hack and the services of a negro driver. The day was bright and warm. The recent rains had cleared the air and clothed the knolls with fresh verdure. Monticello was five miles away. Our road led through Charlottesville. It is an old Virginia town, with old Virginia manners and customs. Northern fingers have scarcely touched it. There are no Queen Anne cottages, no dudes in blazers, and no dashing of equippages. Handsome girls ride through the streets on horseback, attended by cavaliers in black felt hats and top boots. All the white men and women seem born to the saddle. There seem to be more blacks than whites. The houses, though lacking ornament are embowered in roses and Virginia creepers. The churches are also quaint old structures. Sandy and narrow are the streets, and there is general lack of paint in the stores and hotels. It is a peaceful little place. Aside from the equestrians everything has a sleepy look. The negroes move listlessly, and the children seem to play without life. As the place escaped assault and pillage in the war, it presents about the same appearance now as it did when Jefferson died. The Chinaman is the only starling innovation. And he cloaks himself under the old Dominion name of Lee. "Ah Lee" and "Sing Lee" are the laundrymen of the town.

Down Vinegar Hill we drove. It is a locality familiar to students of the University. Monticello came into view as we emerged from the town. It is perched upon a little mountain from which it derives its name—cello, little, and monte, mountain. Mountain peaks could be seen in every direction. The road is shaded with locust and walnut trees. It is very sinuous. The red banks lining the cuts recalled the roads of New Jersey. It was flanked by orchards and meadows dotted with daisies and buttercups. Nature teemed with life. Gaudy dragon flies darted above us, and wasps circled around the mud holes. Crows were sailing above a magnificent wheat field on the left, filling the air with their cries. Robins were picking up insects in the huge bed of plantains, and a pair of mocking birds were loading an old elm with music.

After crossing Moore's Creek, a tributary of the Rivanna, we approached the mountain. A rich vineyard nestled at the foot. As we began to make the ascent, hedges of sassafras, sumach, and scrub oak appeared, with fringes of blackberry and pokeberry bushes. Over them all clambered vines of wild grape. The shadows in the woods grew deeper. A mountain stream, bordered with ferns and nettles, dashed across the road. Half-way up the hill a crystal spring gushed with cooling water beneath the roots of a gigantic oak. Here Jefferson frequently slacked his thirst while riding up and down the mountain.

A few rods further beneath the forest trees and we reached the gap between Monticello and Carter's Mountain. There was an arched wooden gateway at our left. It was the entrance to Monticello. It had been freshly painted, and it looked like the gate of a pretentious country cemetery. Within there was a small porter's lodge. An aged darkey with white locks and wrinkled face, approached us through a postern gate. He pointed to a printed handbill, which informed us that 25 cents was the price of admission. The old negro said that his name was Willis Shelton. He wore scraggy top boots and an old linen duster, a bandana hankerchief was wound around his neck, and he was bareheaded. He held an old gourd toward us to receive the fee.

"Who gets this money?" He was asked, as a silver dollar was dropped into the gourd.

"Massa Levy," he replied.

"Who is Mr. Levy?" was the next query.

"De gemman what owns de place am Massa Levy. De money am his."

"We thought that Mr. Jefferson owned the place?"

Uncle Willis looked surprised. "My, my!" he exclaimed. "Dat were a long time agone—'deed it were. Massa Jefferson's gone and dead many, many years aback."

"Did you know Mr. Jefferson?" was the next inquiry.

"No, sah; not quite," was the answer. "He gone dead 'fore my time"

"Were you not raised at Monticello?"

"Oh, no sah. Mr. Rives, he raised me. I belonged to Mr. Rives before de wah."

"Then you must have known Miss Amelie?"[3]

The reference to the authoress of "The Quick or the Dead?" brought a look of joy to the old man's face. "Does you know Miss 'Melia?" he asked. "She's a angel—'deed she is. Many an' many a time I seen her an' tote her in dese yer black arms."

It was hard to get him to drop Miss Amelia and return to Monticello. Although raised in the family of her uncle, he seemed to have as much affection for her as one of her own servants. Uncle Willis had no idea of his own age. He thought he had been acting as porter there from thirty to thirty-five years. When asked whether money would admit us to Jefferson's house, he replied, "Oh, no, sah. Indeed, Massa Levy won't allow it. You can't go into the house by no means whatsomedever."

We took from him a card of admission. He opened the arched gate and the ascent was continued. It was a winding roadway fringed with bear grass. There was no trace of the bridle paths left by Jefferson. The forest was wild and the trees untrimmed.

Near the top of the hill we reached the cemetery containing the remains of Jefferson and many of his relatives. It is a plot about a hundred feet square, surrounded by an iron railing fully ten feet high. There is a gilt escutcheon upon the iron gate. It carries a lion rampant and three heads of lions upon a shield. Jefferson's grave is nearby, but no one is admitted to the yard. Vandals had despoiled the tomb in former years, and disfigured its obelisk. A new shaft ten feet high, erected by the State of Virginia[4] stands at its head. . . .

After climbing the hill forty rods we emerged from the woods upon the mountain plateau. A five-barred gate admitted us into a young peach orchard. Turkeys and chicken were chasing grasshoppers in the green beneath the trees. A dilapidated negro cabin stood upon our right. An isolated chimney beyond it marks the site of Jefferson's nail factory. Threading our way through the peach orchard, we came to a small park enclosed with wire. There were deer within it. Horses and mules were browsing on the swar[d]s outside. A peacock stood upon a post nearby making a shrill call for more rain, unmindful of the 6,000 victims in the Conamaugh valley.

The plain covers several acres. It is elliptic, and was formed by leveling the apex of the mountain. The waste earth was thrown into a terraced garden below it. It was once filled with the choicest plants and fruit trees. It now contains garden truck and a few thrifty grape vines. The lawn is of surpassing beauty. It was dotted with white clover and mushrooms.

The mansion itself needs no description. Its portico is as familiar to American eyes as the portico of Mount Vernon. Covered ways connect it with the servants' quarters, the weaving house, and other buildings. The servants' quarters are of brick. They stretch from the house in wings, the same as the quarters of the students of the University of Virginia. The plans in both were those of Jefferson. There is a grove of locusts fronting the long low brick building reserved for the servants. The mansion stands in the shade of magnificent lindens brought from France. Most of the trees upon the lawn were planted by the statesman. Among them are a black beech and a copper beech, both brought from France. There is also the remains of a venerable Lombardy poplar, imported from Europe. It is over ninety years old. It is said that from this tree have sprung all the trees of that species in this country.

The view from the lawn is one never to be forgotten. The red farm[s] along the Rivanna and other streams, are spread out below like the map of a surveyor. You see Jefferson's birthplace three miles away among the hills of Shadwell. Charlottesville is to the left, and beyond it the gleaming roofs of the University of Virginia. A sea of foliage and fertile farms stretches toward the South. On the west the blue ridge softens the horizon for a hundred miles or more. Rolling plains and isolated mountains fill in the space below them. One of the eminences is known as Still House Mountain. The captive troops of Sir John Burgoyne were sent here after their surrender at Saratoga.

Between Charlottesville and the Rivanna you see the field where General Marion's old foe, Colonel Tarleton, was encamped in June,

1781. Jefferson was then Governor of Virginia, and the Legislature was in session at Charlottesville. Cornwallis, who was cornered at Yorktown three months later, sent Tarleton to capture Governor Jefferson. A Virginia farmer, getting an inkling of his design, mounted a blooded mare, and reached Charlottesville in time to give the alarm. Tarleton caught seven members of the Legislature early in the morning. The others escaped. Jefferson was at Monticello entertaining the Speaker and several members of the Assembly at breakfast, his servants saw the British crossing Moore's Creek and pushing their way up the mountain. Jefferson and his family made their escape ten minutes before Tarleton's dragoons reached the gate at the gap, now kept by Willis Shelton. . . .

The agent who received our tickets strenuously refused to allow us to enter the house. He said that Mr. Levy forbade it and that was enough. He conducted us to a bow window at the end of the portico and pointed out the chair in which he said Thomas Jefferson sat when he wrote the Declaration of Independence. It is a plain black wooden chair with a writing-board attachment. The Declaration, however, was not written at Monticello. Jefferson says that he wrote it at his lodgings in the house of Mrs. Cirmer,[5] on the southwest corner of Seventh and High Streets, Philadelphia.

There is really little to see in the mansion. The furniture used by the Jefferson family has disappeared. Mr. Levy, the owner, has, however, spared the interior of the house. He has not altered the rooms. His agent pointed out the separate bedrooms of Mr. and Mrs. Jefferson. They are joined by an alcove. In days of yore the bed in which both slept occupied this alcove. Mrs. Jefferson entered the bed from her own room, where she was joined by her husband, who crept into the cot from his private apartment.

The agent went into ecstacies over a carved marble mantel which he did not exhibit. He said that it was ornamented with exquisite figures upon a blue ground. He also pointed out Mr. Levy's ice house, where Jefferson formerly made his brick. The only notable curiosity left was a plaster cast of the head of a pillar designed by Jefferson for use in the Capitol at Washington; it is of a purely American order of architecure and was meant to take the place of Corinthian pillars. The leaves and blossoms of the tobacco plant are grouped on the head of the pillar, instead of the acanthus.

The bricks used in the mansion and in the outbuildings were made from the red clay of the mountain. Jefferson utilized raw material. The nails were forged a stone's throw from his library, and the cloth used to clothe his servants was woven in a building near the negro quarters.

The Levy purchase includes a little more than 200 acres. It is said to have been bought for $10,000. The old estate covered 3,700 acres, and was cultivated by 113 slaves. Jefferson's pecuniary troubles date from the time of his embargo proclamation. For eight years and until the close of the war of 1812, there was very little demand for grain and tobacco. His estates were managed by overseers who lacked prudence and foresight. They ran him into debt. On retiring from the Presidency he borrowed $10,000 to pay his debts. This however, did not suffice. He dispensed lavish hospitality at Monticello, and his debts increased. The crisis was reached when he endorsed the note of a friend for $20,000. The friend failed to meet its payment, and Jefferson saw bankruptcy before him. The Legislature of Virginia gave him permission to dispose of part of his land by lottery. He fancied that he could thus pay his debts and retain Monticello. Much sympathy was expressed for him when this scheme was broached. Philip Hone, then Mayor of New York, raised $8,500, and mayors of other cities increased the sum to $17,000. The raising of this sum, however, increased Mr. Jefferson's difficulties. It was totally inadequate for his necessities, and it virtually suppressed the lottery scheme. At this juncture Mr. Jefferson died. His estates were sold to liquidate his debts.

It is said the Monticello twice changed owners, and then fell into the possession of Captain Levy, father of the present owner. This may be so, but I am told that Captain Levy bought the estate at the request of Andrew Jackson. However this may be, it is certain that Monticello is now owned by a Levy, who charges patriotic Americans, Democrat and Republican, twenty-five cents admission to the grounds alone, and refuses admission to the house at any price during his absence. This Levy is named after Jefferson. He has a law office at 25 Nassau Street, and a residence at 66 East Thirty-fourth Street, New York, City. It is proper to add that he is said to be persistently seeking a Democratic nomination for either Congress or the Assembly. His friends say that he is now in Europe, the guest of North, the English nitrate king.

The latest Levy is said to value Monticello at $100,000. Possibly he imagines that he can eventually sell it to either the State or the Federal Government for this sum. If so, the bargain ought soon to be consummated. Time is destroying the trees and outbuildings, and the mansion itself is decaying.

Amos J. Cummings, *A National Humiliation* (n.p., 1902).

1. The story is untrue.

2. The great flood of May 1889.

3. Amélie Rives Chanler Troubetzkoy (1863–1945) grew up at nearby Castle Hill, in Cobham, owned by her grandparents.

4. In fact, erected by Congress.

5. The house was that of Jacob Graff.

1912

A Pilgrim Turns Crusader

MAUD LITTLETON, the Texan-born wife of a prominent New York congressman, first visited Monticello in 1909. Shocked to discover more of Levy than of Jefferson in the mansion, she launched a crusade to make Monticello a national shrine. An association was formed and dedicated to this purpose. Taking as her motto Jefferson's moving line, "All my wishes end where I hope my days will end, at Monticello," Mrs. Littleton made a strong bid for public support. In addition to her writings, such as the pamphlet *One Wish*, she testified at length before committees of Congress. This excerpt is from her testimony before the House Rules Committee in 1912.

EVER SINCE I WAS BORN I have been hearing of Monticello, and my parents had always promised me a trip there, that they would either take me or send me to Monticello. Virginia was a long way from Texas in those days, but nobody ever left home without stopping off at Charlottesville. And they continue to do so to this day.

When I was there a few days ago, in answer to inquiries, I was told that the trains never stop at Charlottesville without people getting off and hiring carriages to drive up the mountain to where Jefferson is buried, and that an average of 60 people a day visit his home. Most of the tourists visiting Washington think nothing of taking the train over to see Monticello—that is a part of their plan and trip.

Monticello has been in my thought ever since I first saw it. I remember it was about three years ago when I accompanied my husband to Virginia where he made the founder's day address at the university.

Aerial view of Monticello, 1978. Photograph by Ed Roseberry

We stopped at the home of Dr. Alderman, president of the university, and Mrs. Alderman, and one night we were invited by Mr. Levy to dine at Monticello. Friends advised us not to go on account of the roads. But I begged. Had I not heard of Mount Vernon and Monticello all my life? When I was a child in Texas, was it not a great event when people traveled as far away by train as Virginia to visit Mount Vernon and Monticello. And didn't I watch for their home-coming to hear beautiful stories about it all?

I remember that night, three years ago, when Mr. Levy invited us to dinner. Somehow it did not enter my mind that I was going to visit him. He did not seem to me to be a part of Monticello. Thomas Jefferson was uppermost in my mind; I could think of no one else. Somehow I had never connected Mr. Levy with Mr. Jefferson and Monticello. He had not entered my dreams.

Well, the evening came, and we drove through the black night and deep mud up that steep road to the top of the little mountain. Nothing could be seen. Only above our heads a thick mass of bare limbs of trees, like serpents coiled above us. I can remember nothing now of the house and my visit, except that I have a vivid impression of portraits—big oil portraits of the Levys—and ships—models of ships in which Uriah Levy was supposed to have sailed.

I did not get the feeling of being in the house Thomas Jefferson built and loved and made sacred, and of paying a tribute to him. I did not seem to feel his spirit hovering around those portraits. My heart sunk. My dream was spoiled. Jefferson seemed detached from Monticello. He seemed to have been brushed to one side and to be fading into a dim tradition. Somebody else was taking his place in Monticello—an outsider. A rank outsider.

Everything was disappointing. I had a heavy-hearted feeling. There was nothing of Jefferson to me at Monticello. He had dropped out and the Levys had come. One could hear and see only the Levys and the Levy family, their deeds of valor, their accomplishments, their lives. And I wished that I could get them out of my mind, but when I left Monticello Thomas Jefferson was but a disappearing memory, run out into and mixed up with the Levys.

I made up my mind to find out how it all came about. It seemed to me that the people of the United States should own Monticello; that it should be public property like Mount Vernon; that it should not be lived in by anybody or used as a summer home; that it should be open the year round so that people who make long journeys to get there could go in and see it; that it should not be for just those few who were fortunate enough to know Mr. Levy and to have special invitations from him, but that everybody should be free to go there; that it should be furnished as much like Mr. Jefferson had it as possible, and that it should not stand as a memorial to any other human being.

Statement of Mrs. Littleton before the House Rules Committee, July 24, 1912, *Congressional Record,* 62 Cong., 2d Sess., Appendix, 859.

⊰ 1924 ⊱

⌡

An Architect's
View

COINCIDING WITH the movement before the First World War
to make Monticello a national shrine was Jefferson's growing
reputation as an architect and of Monticello as an architectural masterpiece. The man most responsible for this was the
architect and historian Fiske Kimball, whose magnum opus,
Thomas Jefferson, Architect, was published in 1916. After the
Thomas Jefferson Memorial Foundation acquired the property, Kimball was placed in charge of its restoration. Meanwhile, he had become director of the Philadelphia Museum of
Art. Kimball offered his professional view of Monticello in a
brief article published in the *Journal of the American Institute
of Architects* in 1924.

MONTICELLO, the home of Jefferson, is set on a mountain top. To us,
heirs of the romanticism of which he was the American pioneer, there
is nothing strange in this, but in his day it was wholly new, even in
Europe. From his boyhood home in the watered valley, his spirit
yearned toward the heights, with that profound reverence for nature
to which he once gave expression at a prospect in the Alpes Mari-
times: "Fall down and worship . . . you never saw, nor will ever see
such another." From Monticello itself there unrolls on the west a
mountain panorama of the Blue Ridge scarcely less magnificent, while
to the east stretches the endless plain, his "sea view," as he called it.

Here, when scarce out of college, he dreamed of creating, in what
was then still wilderness, natural gardens with cascades, enriched by
temples Greek and Gothic—the first American landscape garden. Like

the young Goethe, whose youthful panegyric on the cathedral of Strassburg was then soon to appear, Jefferson began as a thorough romantic.

Like Goethe too, however—in this as in so many other respects— Jefferson soon turned to the classic. In his own final judgment, witnessed by his epitaph, he appears above all as a lover of freedom, whether in politics, in religion, or in science; but the freedom thus loved from youth was essentially the freedom of reason to reach its logical conclusions, not freedom to degenerate into formless anarchy. Trained in the law, he demanded logical system in thought. He insisted, too, on going to the sources in every field: in his fundamental study of the common law, in his researches among fossils, in his Biblical criticism. Thus he was led back to the earliest precedents, among the Anglo-Saxons, the Greeks, the Romans.

Thus is explained the paradox that Jefferson, the apostle of individualism, should have chosen as his first master in architecture, Palladio, who passes as the chief representative of dogmatic authority. The reconciliation lies first in the character of reasoned law borne by Palladio's architectural system. However artificial it may seem to us, it had in common with nature this supposed lawfulness and reasonableness, which was doubtless what Palladio himself felt when he wrote: "Architecture, the imitator of Nature." Here was the relation to natural law, one of Jefferson's fundamental conceptions. With the weight of primitive and classic precedent which Palladio sought to adduce and Jefferson was quick to respect, the preponderance of spiritual agreement between them was overwhelming.

Teaching himself to draw—like Washington and like his own father, Peter Jefferson, a surveyor of land—he modelled his designs on the plates of Palladio's work and mastered the grammar of architectural detail with a new insistence on classic correctness. Hundreds of sketches and drawings by his own hand, based on his marginal calculations, are still preserved. The designs for Monticello were essentially fixed, and the first building, Jefferson's study, was already occupied, in 1771, before he sent an appeal to his business correspondent in the Tidewater to get him an architect to supervise the construction. Even then none came. There were none to be had. In all the colonies there was not then a single architect in the professional sense. Hallet and Latrobe, men of fine foreign training, did not emigrate to

America until the last decade of the century. Thornton and Bulfinch, at first gentlemen-amateurs, though now revered as fathers of the profession, did not begin their architectural careers until 1789. Robert Mills, to whom the design of Monticello has sometimes been ascribed, was still unborn. The drawings of the colonial master-builders, still preserved, are childish beside Jefferson's. Only old Peter Harrison at Newport, himself always an amateur, and Hawks, Governor Tryon's man, had made such drawings here before him. At that time, we learn, there were not two stonemasons in the whole county of Albemarle. Jefferson had to train his own workmen, and created a body of them that spread his ideas in the magnificent houses all up and down the South.

The house which Jefferson built at Monticello for his young bride was something then new in America. It was not merely an unadorned pile like the old buildings at Harvard College or at William and Mary, of which Jefferson wrote, "but that they have roofs, would be taken for brick kilns." Nor was it adorned with a "burden of barbarous ornaments," as Jefferson called the scroll pediments and other baroque features of the colonial houses of the James River and Annapolis. "To give these symmetry and taste," he wrote, "would not increase their cost. It would only change the arrangement of the materials, the form and combination of the members." Thus Jefferson taught the great truth that the supreme merit in architecture lies in geometrical simplicity and proportion. From this point of view, we can understand the enthusiasm of foreign travelers like the Duc de la Rochefoucauld-Liancourt, who said Jefferson was the first American to consult the arts on how to shelter himself from the weather.

As we see it today, Monticello is not as Jefferson first designed it and the Marquis of Chastellux saw it just after the Revolution. Then it was thinner and higher, with a great library in the centre upstairs, attics over the wings, and a second portico over the first, like the Venetian villas of Palladio along the Brenta. Liancourt saw its reconstruction begun in 1796, and wrote: "Monticello, according to its first plan, was infinitely superior to all other houses in America, in point of taste and convenience; but at that time Mr. Jefferson had studied taste and the fine arts in books only. His travels in Europe have supplied him with models; he had appropriated them to his design; and his new plan . . . will be accomplished . . . and then his house will certainly deserve to be ranked with the most pleasant houses of England and France." At Nîmes, as he wrote the Comtesse de Tessé, he had gazed "whole hours at the Maison Quarrée, like a lover at his mistress"; in Paris he was "violently smitten with the Hotel de Salm, and used to go to the Tuileries almost daily to look at it"; in Southern France he was "immersed in antiquities from morning to night." It was to make his house more truly Roman that he removed the upper story and attic, and built instead, on the lines of the Hotel de Salm, the Roman Dome which we see.

This was the Jefferson to whom we owe the superbly classic form of the early buildings of the Republic: The Virginia Capitol, for which he himself made the drawings and had the model made in Paris; the competition of the public buildings in Washington, the first great public competition among architects in America, of which, as Secretary of State, he wrote the program, and in which he himself submitted a design; the encouragement, when he was President, of the first trained architects from abroad, to establish, amid inconceivable difficulties, the profession and the art of architecture. This was the man who sent Houdon to Virginia to make the portrait of Washington, who brought sculptors from Italy, who imported carvings from Carrara. He deserves to be known, not only as author of the Declaration of Independence, but as the father of the arts in America.

Jefferson, the architect and patron of art, was far ahead of his time. To Philistines of the day any dabbling in the arts was beneath the attention of a public man, and at best they looked on his activity with good natured tolerance. At worst, partisanship invented absurd canards like those of Callendar. When Jefferson took his stairway out of the entrance hall, and gave the stairs privacy in a house overrun with unbidden guests, it said the "philosopher" had forgotten the stairs. When he placed the kitchens in a basement, below a terrace from which one enjoyed the superb panorama, people said the corridor below was an underground passage built to escape from the British.

It can easily be understood that Monticello as it stands today should be a trifle disappointing. When a swarm of guests and their horses were eating Jefferson into bankruptcy in his later years, rooms had to be improvised in the cornices, the roof had to be raised and filled with garret dormers.[1] The house was under almost constant reconstruction. Jefferson took it cheerfully, saying to a visitor: "So I hope it will remain during my life, as architecture is my delight, and putting up, and pulling down one of my favorite amusements." Then, in the long period of neglect and litigation in the middle of the last century, much disappeared, and the beautiful furniture brought from Paris was largely dispersed. In recent years decay has set in in some places: one can no longer walk the terraces; some of the magnificent trees are yielding to old age. There are a few incongruous additions.

But the main fabric stands unharmed, and at every point we have Jefferson's own drawings and notes, so that all could be put back in beauty precisely as it was. Every tree and bush he planted is located and marked. The place waits only to be reclaimed by the nation and restored with loving hands.

In Spring, when the Virginia woods are ablaze with the flowering shrubs and trees Jefferson loved, when the hills are golden with the broom he first planted, when the air is heavy with the scent of locust, then at Monticello we can even now recapture the magic of Jefferson's artistry. We fall under the spell of this great man, the very founder of American Democracy, and worship at his grave and at his shrine, a shrine of a whole nation.

Fiske Kimball, "Monticello," *Journal of American Institute of Architects* 12 (1924): 175–81. Reprinted by permission of The American Institute of Architects Archives.

1. This was actually a Levy innovation.

⁓⁂ 1 9 5 4 ⁂⁓

ʃ

After the
Overhaul

FOR THE FIRST TIME since it was opened to the public, Monticello closed for major repairs during the winter months of 1953–54. In the course of the renovation much was learned about the inner structure and workings of the house. Some mysteries were unraveled; some myths were laid to rest once and for all. A reporter for the *New York Times*, F. John Long, filed the following article on the eve of the reopening. It is worth preserving because it treats an important chapter in the history of the house, though one may take exception to his labeling Monticello a "colonial mansion," let alone likening it to a contemporary ranch house.

MONTICELLO, the home of Thomas Jefferson, will open to the public again tomorrow after four months, during which the historic mansion underwent the most complete renovation job in its more than a century and a half of existence.

The $240,000 overhaul was long overdue. Like the White House, venerable Monticello had been patched and propped and jury-rigged for many years. In January, 1953, when one of the bedroom floors sagged and nearly collapsed, it was obvious that the time had come for drastic action. Exterior repair work started on July 6, and the mansion itself was closed to visitors on November 15.

Unlike the White House restoration, however, no more of Monticello was dismantled than was absolutely necessary, and [not] much of the original brick and lumber was replaced. The basic procedure was somewhat like that followed at Mount Vernon a number of years ago when steel girders and new oak shoring were notched through old hand-hewn beams no longer able to support their burdens. In this way the beautiful original flooring, still in good condition, and the ceilings were undisturbed.

The Jefferson Memorial Foundation, which operates Monticello as a patriotic, non-profit corporation, placed the project in the hands of its architect, Milton L. Grigg, one of the nation's top authorities on Colonial homes, and R. E. Lee Jr., a Charlottesville engineer-contractor. Mr. Grigg was given a free hand by Fiske Kimball, chairman of the restoration committee of the foundation, but the guiding precept was: "Preserve rather than restore, and restore rather than reconstruct."

One of the most important phases of the renovation program was the installation of a modern air-conditioning system. This serves three purposes, the primary one being the reduction of the humidity that caused so much damage to woodwork and furniture. Its second function is to heat the house in winter, a task formerly done by unsightly and dangerous portable oilstoves (unknown in Jefferson's day). The third purpose is summer cooling, although the temperature will be reduced only a few degrees below that outdoors.

A marvelous job of concealing ventilating ducts has been done. The visitor may never notice the small openings, half-hidden by woodwork, mirror frames, curtains and pictures, that introduce a constant flow of dehumidified air. Fireplace flues return the air to the air-conditioning unit, the chimneys being sealed at the top.

Jefferson, who made many changes in the mansion during the forty years he owned Monticello . . . unwittingly helped the engineers who placed the air ducts when he made and later bricked up certain openings and niches in the walls. Some of these were found and cleaned out to carry pipes and wiring, thus requiring no structural alterations.

"In fact, the entire chronology of Monticello will have to be rewritten as a result of the findings made during the renovation," Mr. Grigg said. "Jefferson, we know, undertook two major reconstruction jobs, but we also discovered evidence of several intermediate stages. I think we can now make a really complete archaeological report, based on sound evidence rather than conjecture."

A total of eighty steel "I" beams, the longest seventeen feet, were slotted into the original timbers supporting the flooring. First some of

100 tons of rubble or nogging (a filler of plaster, bricks and stone) had to be removed. This nogging served as sound-proofing, as a firebreak and for temperature control, but it harbored both dampness and termites. It has been replaced with metal lathes and fire-resistant materials.

With its temple-like dome and Doric porticos, Monticello looks larger than it actually is. However, it might be called the nation's first "ranch-type" house, because all of the important rooms are on a single floor. There are two floors of sleeping chambers above the first, but Jefferson used them chiefly for housing unexpected guests and the children of the family. Monticello alone of important colonial mansions had no grand staircase—only two narrow back stairs. Visitors who ask how ladies in hoopskirts managed them are informed by well-versed lady guides at Monticello that hoopskirts were not known in Jefferson's day!

The Monticello renovation was expected to reveal some secrets about the ingenious gadgets with which Jefferson filled the mansion but which he never bothered to describe in his papers. And it did. At the same time some legends, so well accepted by visitors that they have been incorporated in standard reference books, were deflated.

Monticello's prime mystery, until this year, was the mechanism that operated the double glass doors between the large reception hall and the drawing room. Both opened or closed when only one of them was pushed, but no one knew exactly how. When workmen removed the nogging beneath the first floor they found that each door was swung on a concealed drum. The drums were connected by two hand wrought sprocket chains, somewhat similar to a bicycle chain. Midway the chains crossed, turning the drums in the opposite direction with the movement of either door. This amazingly simple mechanism is still in perfect condition.

Perhaps the legend that will be hardest to down concerns Jefferson's bed, in an alcoved opening between his dressing room and study.

"Shortly after the foundation took over the mansion in 1923," according to Mr. Grigg, "a story began to go around that the bed had once been suspended on ropes from pulleys, and was drawn up out of the way during the daylight hours. In a little room above the bed, it was said, slept Jefferson's bodyguard and man-servant.

"The foundation never took much stock in the story, but couldn't disprove it. The public relished it, it was widely printed, and had been recorded as fact in some of the writing about Monticello. But probing within the walls and ceiling during the renovation has decisively proved that the bedframe was hooked to the walls of the alcove, and that the small room above was used as a closet for boots, uniforms, etc. Pulleys near the ceiling of the bedroom probably operated the skylight."

Another ancient legend recounts Jefferson's narrow escape from capture at Monticello by British patrols in June, 1781. As the story goes, Jefferson galloped his horse to safety through a basement tunnel as the raiders broke in the front door. But no tunnel has yet been found large enough to clear a man on horseback.

In the basement several rooms, including those used for the storage of wine and beer, have now been cleaned out and painted. Here, too, will be a repository of relics, furniture, books and other memorabilia not being used for display. . . .

Despite the loss of one and one-half months, 1953 was a good year for visitors to Monticello. According to Superintendent Curtis Thacker, attendance totaled 232,000. The most crowded day was October 22, with 2,200 visitors.

ᴀ 1 9 5 6 ᴘ

ʃ

Homage of a
Third-World Leader

THE HOMAGE President Sukarno of Indonesia paid to Jefferson at Monticello in 1956 was a remarkable testament to the Virginian's global influence. A leader of his people's struggle for independence from the Netherlands and the first president of the new republic of Indonesia after World War II, Sukarno, unfortunately, proved unfaithful to the principles of his "great teacher" and was overthrown some years later. This dispatch was written by Tillman Durdin for the *New York Times*.

CHARLOTTESVILLE, VA., MAY 20—President Sukarno of Indonesia paid homage to Thomas Jefferson here today.

He described a visit to Monticello, the beautiful hilltop home of the author of the Declaration of Independence, as a pilgrimage to honor "my great teacher."

Most of Dr. Sukarno's fifth day of a nineteen-day state visit to the United States was spent amid scenes connected with the life and ideals of the third President of the United States.

Indonesia's Moslem chief of state placed a wreath on Jefferson's tomb. Then, with eyes closed and hands raised in solemn invocation, he murmured an Islamic prayer.

He said later that he had asked God "to give Jefferson the best place in Heaven."

In an extemporaneous address at a luncheon given in his honor by the Thomas Jefferson Memorial Foundation, Dr. Sukarno said Jefferson's life and ideas had been an inspiration to him during the years when he struggled for the independence of Indonesia.

He said Jefferson's view on freedom and the independence of peoples had set a "big fire burning in Indonesia."

"In Indonesia we are implementing the great idea put forward by Thomas Jefferson," Dr. Sukarno asserted. "So, my pilgrimage today was not only a pilgrimage performed by Sukarno. I performed a pilgrimage as Sukarno representing the Indonesian people."

He declared Jefferson's fire would continue to burn until "all the people in the world are free, until all the people in the world are united in a great brotherhood of man, until all the people of the world are living in a pax humanica."

Noting that Jefferson was great because "in him lived a great idea," he lauded President Eisenhower and said that he also was great, not because he was a good soldier or a good President, but "because in him lives a great idea."

He reminded his audience that he had come to the United States to look for "a state of mind" and said that he had found it already "centered here in Virginia, where my great teacher, Jefferson, lived."

"Sukarno Homage Paid to Jefferson," *New York Times,* May 21, 1956. Copyright © 1956 by The New York Times Company. Reprinted by permission.

∫

"Our Man Stanley"
at Monticello

"OUR MAN STANLEY," the peripatetic correspondent for *The New Yorker,* went to Monticello as an ordinary tourist in 1958. He picked up the southern tone of the presentation of the house—much more evident then than now—and wrote an amusing column about it. "Our man Stanley" was Philip Hamburger, who included this piece in a book with that title in 1963.

OUR MAN STANLEY stopped by the office the other day, remarked, "All men may be created equal, but we shall not look upon his like again," and deposited the following dispatch:

"Have been in Charlottesville, Virginia, visiting friends, and went to Monticello, home of Thomas Jefferson, to pay respects to memory of great man and see house. *Some* house! No split-level ranch-type house this! Paid dollar fee at gatehouse at foot of steep hill, was handed ticket, and drove to pinnacle, with car sandwiched between bus loaded with ladies from Winnebago, Minnesota, garden clubs and bus loaded with children from Louisa County public schools. Breathtaking view from top—hazy Blue Ridge rising above Piedmont to one side, broad green Tidewater to other. Grounds aflame with flowers; ancient tulip poplars and lindens all over place. Entered red brick house with white Doric columns through east portico, along with Winnebago ladies, schoolchildren. Ticket taken by distinguished-looking colored man of advanced years, in blue uniform. 'Mornin',' he said. Had feeling he probably worked for Jefferson.

"Crowds fell silent in entrance hall, looking every which way—at clock above door, with cluster of cannon-ball weights hanging on each side wall (days of week marked on south wall; each day southern cluster descends to next day's mark), at brass lamp hanging from ceiling, at stylized plaster eagle on ceiling, at French doors leading to drawing room beyond. 'Mornin',' said a distinguished-looking woman. 'If you-all would care to follow me, I will show you through parts of Mistuh Jefferson's house. The antlers that you see beside the clock were gifts to Mistuh Jefferson from Lewis and Clark at the time of their celebrated expedition to the West. It took two years to level the top of this mountain for Mistuh Jefferson, and that lamp there burned Whale oil. [Winnebago lady: 'Whale oil?' Guide: 'Yes, Ma'am, whale oil. Oil from whales.'] Mistuh Jefferson had fifty-seven house servants, thirty-five rooms, and ten acres of lawn. Mistuh Jefferson was his own architect. He had no builder, and no finished material except what was made on the place. Mistuh Jefferson often had fifty guests—some invited, some uninvited.' Had impression Mr. Jefferson was somewhere around house, hiding from guests.

"Followed lady through fine, quiet, high-ceilinged rooms. Never saw so much Chippendale, Wedgwood, Waterford glass, Lowestoft china, detail work on mantels, doors, ceilings, balconies. Jefferson great gadget man—revolving chair and worktable, music rack designed for five players' simultaneous use, dumbwaiter in dining room to bring wine bottles from cellar, revolving buffet that looks like door on one side, keeps food from kitchen warm on other. Learned that Mr. Jefferson put in first storm windows in this country, also first parquet floors—cherry and beech. Doors connecting entrance hall and drawing room most ingenious. First bus-type doors in America; both doors open at same time. Lady said doors haven't been oiled in one hundred fifty-eight years. Until three years ago, everybody thought doors operated by complicated, arcane lever system. During repairs, discovered devilishly clever, simple arrangement of bicycle-type chains attached to drums at pivots of doors.

"Said 'Mornin' ' to guide, Winnebago ladies, and children, and ducked out of house down to all-weather passageway connecting service areas beneath north and south terraces and house itself. Saw Cyder Room—'I will be glad to take of you the present year about 90 or 100 gallons of cyder,' said Jefferson quotation over door. Saw Wine Room—'No nation is drunken when wine is cheap; and none sober when the dearness of wine substitutes ardent spirits,' said Jefferson quotation. Saw Beer Cellar—'I wish to see this beverage become common, instead of the whiskey which kills one-third of our citizens,' said Jefferson quotation. Puttered around museum, off passageway, which displayed Jefferson's spectacles, shoe buckles, slippers worn under silk hose, miscroscope, palette, paintbox, plans for moldboard, ivory memorandum tablets, gold toothpick, and invitation card for dinner ('half after three o'clock'). Peeked into old kitchen, separated from main house, food having been run through passageway to warming kitchens. Saw cabbage slicer, coffee mill, tons of pots, pans, caldrons, real cabbage, real eggs, huge onions, apples. Mr. Jefferson apparently expecting guests. Saw smokehouse, saw pond where fish were kept alive until dinnertime, saw Jefferson's Honeymoon Cottage, where he brought his bride in 1772, on horseback, through eighteen inches of snow. Walked around grounds and admired plinths on dome, and Doric columns, and details of soffit, mutules, guttae, interspaces, and triglyphs.

"Ran into lady guide again, standing on portico, taking breather. 'We had two hundred and sixty-three thousand paid visitors in 1957,' she said. 'No one under twelve pays. We're open every single day of the year. We've had more than two thousand on a Sunday, and there will be a steady thousand a day every single day all through June. People from Charlottesville and Albemarle County do not pay. Every time I go through Mistuh Jefferson's house, I see something new. The staircases are only twenty-four inches wide, so we don't let visitors upstairs. The Sky Room, on the top, was to have been used by Mistuh Jefferson for billiards, but billiards were forbidden in Virginia by the time the house was completed. Mistuh Jefferson did not give balls. He had a telescope on the roof. He and James Madison exchanged weather reports for many years. Mistuh Madison was from Orange County. The basement walls are sixteen inches thick. The key to the clock in the hall looks like an automobile crank. Hickory-smoked hams are sold on the place, also seeds of white globe amaranth and hollyhock from the Monticello gardens. I guess this is the most beautiful place in the world.' Said goodbye to lady, and to Mr. Jefferson, and departed."

From *Our Man Stanley* (Bobbs-Merrill). © 1958, 1986 Philip Hamburger. Originally in *The New Yorker* 34 (1958): 23–24.

~~⟨ 1 9 8 4 ⟩~~

ʃ

"An Old Man . . .
but a Young Gardener"

IN RECENT YEARS Jefferson has been recognized as a distinguished architect of landscapes as well as of buildings—
above all as a passionate gardener. Ongoing research and restoration at Monticello have contributed to the rising interest
in this dimension of Jefferson's genius. Richard L. Williams, a
contributing editor of the *Smithsonian,* surveyed this devel-
opment during a visit to the mountain in 1984.

WHEN THOMAS JEFFERSON was a young law clerk he enjoyed striding
about the Virginia hilltop his father had bequeathed to him, thinking
grandly of the fine home and gardens that he would someday create
there. He had not yet been to Italy, but already he had in mind the
idea of christening the place Monticello and pronouncing the "little
mountain" *montichel'lo* in the Italian way. It took Jefferson the better
part of 60 years to make his dreams come true, mainly because he had
so many distractions to contend with—as author of the Declaration
of Independence, as American Minister to France, as George Washington's Secretary of State, as a two-term President of the United States
and as founder of the University of Virginia.

Jefferson was the quintessential man of many parts. It was his for-
midable intellect that enabled him to accomplish so much in public
life. His superb architectural sensibilities were responsible for the elegant innovations of the mansion that he built at Monticello. But it
was a lesser-known attribute, his green thumb, that accounted for the
splendid horticultural accomplishments that were on display at Jefferson's estate—broad lawns, glorious flower beds, innovative orchards

and vineyards, and a spectacular vegetable garden that was longer than three of today's football fields placed end to end. In addition to all of his other extraordinary gifts, Thomas Jefferson was one of the most inventive gardeners of his time.

Cultivating the soil was not just a hobby with Jefferson; it was a passion. "I am become the most *ardent* farmer in the state," he proudly announced in middle age. As an old man, he wrote to his longtime friend, the artist Charles Willson Peale, that "Under a total want of demand except for our family table, I am still devoted to the garden. Though an old man, I am but a young gardener." In the same letter he told the painter that "No occupation is so delightful to me as the culture of the earth, and no culture comparable to that of the garden. Such a variety of subjects, some one always coming to perfection, the failure of one thing repaired by the success of another, and instead of one harvest a continued one through the year."

Sadly, Jefferson was more than $100,000 in debt when he died in 1826 and his heirs had to abandon Monticello and its gardens to the ravages of time and neglect. But now, almost two centuries after he first laid admiring eyes on the great estate gardens of England, the foundation that bears Jefferson's name is restoring the ones he designed and planted at Monticello. The ambitious project is more than a dramatic lesson in horticultural history. It serves as a living testimonial to Jefferson and a celebration of his well-known preference for the rural life. He was, after all, the Founding Father who fervently believed the cities are "pestilential to the morals, the health and the liberties of men."

In its complexity, the garden task is as challenging as the restoration and refurnishing of the mansion itself, which has been going on for 50-odd years. Several people are in charge of the project. One is William L. Beiswanger, architectural historian of the Thomas Jefferson Memorial Foundation, which owns Monticello and derives most of its income from the $4 admission fee paid by a half million visitors each year. Beiswanger's role is to come up with new restoration ideas and coordinate the work to be done on them. Resident archaeologist William Kelso is assembling evidence on the precise locations of the gardens and buildings that Jefferson supervised at Monticello. Horticulturist Peter Hatch, the gardening superintendent, must decide which variety of fruit tree, ornamental tree, grapevine and vegetable

Jefferson cultivated in the red-clay soil of Albemarle County. The restorers have been helped immensely by the fact that Jefferson, an almost obsessive record keeper, left voluminous notes in his *Garden Book*, his *Farm Book* and in a memorandum book that told whom he owed and who owed him. But he also left gaps in the record, so that the restoration people are sometimes on their own when it comes to deciding which species to replant, and where to plant them.

Jefferson's father had died in 1757 when Thomas was only 14, leaving him 5,000 acres of land, including the little mountain. By the time he was 28, Jefferson was a successful lawyer and apparently he had already decided that he wanted Monticello to be a kind of "ornamented farm" that combined gardens for both pleasure and practicality. This notion was subsequently reinforced by his reading and by his extensive tours of gardens in Europe. He had specific plans for the grounds, as he wrote in a 1771 memorandum: "Thin the trees. Cut out stumps and undergrowth. Remove old trees and other rubbish except where they may look well. Cover the whole with grass. Intersperse Jesamine, honeysuckle, sweetbrier, and even hardy flowers which may not require attention. Keep in it deer, rabbits, Peacocks, Guinea poultry, pidgeons, etc. Let it be an asylum for hares, squirrels, pheasants, partidges, and every other wild animal (except those of prey). Court them to it by laying food for them in proper places. Procure a buck elk, to be, as it were, Monarch of the wood; but keep him shy, that his appearance may not lose its effect by too much familiarity. A buffalo might be confined also. . . ." Much of it was done in time, and Jefferson even had deer eating corn out of his hand.

But first he had to level the top of the little mountain into an elliptical site for the substantial home he would build there. Eventually, the lopped-off hilltop was surrounded by four circuitous roads, or "round-abouts," used for driving or walking. They were connected by oblique roads that cut through the heavy timber. The flower beds around the main house were oval in shape, too. Beyond the house on the west side Jefferson located a lawn, surrounded by a serpentine walk. More flower beds, divided into ten-foot sections, bordered that walk.

Jefferson's granddaughter, Ellen Randolph Coolidge, recalled his affection for Monticello's flowers in a letter written some years after his death: "I remember well when he first returned to Monticello, how immediately he began to prepare new beds for his flowers. . . . I remember the planting of the first hyacinths and tulips, and their subsequent growth. . . . Then, when spring returned, how eagerly we watched the first appearance of the shoots above ground. Each root was marked with its own name written on a bit of stick by its side, and what joy it was for one of us to discover the tender green breaking through the mould, and run to granpapa to announce, that we really believed Marcus Aurelius was coming up, or the Queen of the Amazons was above ground! With how much pleasure compounded of our pleasure and his own, on the new birth, he would immediately go out to verify the fact, and praise us for our diligent watchfulness. Then when the flowers were in bloom, and we were in ecstasies over the rich purple and crimson, or pure white, or delicate lilac, or pale yellow of the blossoms, how he would sympathize in our admiration. . . ."

The horticulturists who are restoring the gardens at Monticello cultivate the species that Jefferson knew about, such as four-o'clocks, rather sparse and leggy ageratum and the Columbian lily (*Fritillaria pudica*) that Lewis and Clark brought back from their Western expedition. In the interests of authenticity, they avoid using flowers that had not yet been developed or imported from Asia, South America and Africa, such as the hybrid delphinium or petunia.

The mansion at Monticello, famous for the kind of restless ingenuity that was Jefferson's trademark, is thought to be the first domed structure in America. The main hall contained Jefferson's great clock, with its descending weights marking off the days of the week. In the dining room Jefferson's system of dumbwaiters enabled guests to receive wine without being interrupted by servants. The same penchant for creative problem solving is exhibited in Monticello's grounds and gardens. The cisterns that augmented the water supply from Monticello's undependable well are of Jefferson's own design. So is the oval pond that he installed as a holding tank for edible fish and also, possibly, as a sometime reservoir for garden water. The pond was located near the southwest pavilion, which was built as his bachelor quarters. Here he and his bride, the former Mrs. Martha Wayles Skelton, spent their first night at Monticello in 1772.

Not far from this pavilion, but out of sight of the mansion, was the plantation village Jefferson called Mulberry Row. Situated beside a thousand-foot stretch of roadway planted with mulberry trees, the row consisted of at least 19 buildings, including slave quarters, the nailery, the joinery and the blacksmith shop. Almost to the very end, Jefferson hoped that some of those enterprises would help Monticello become self-sufficient and thereby ease his burden of debt, but they never did. Today, in an effort to learn more about slave life in Mulberry Row, Kelso and his workers are looking for archaeological evidence where the buildings once stood. They have gathered up hundreds of nails from the nailery, and they have patiently scraped and brushed the earth to uncover bits of crockery, iron tools and bones from cast-off refuse.

Just below Mulberry Row—parallel to it, in fact—Jefferson put his vegetable garden. It was every bit as long as the village roadway, and it was 80 feet wide. In it, Jefferson tried to grow more than 250 varieties—everything from Hotspur peas and a squash called "warted cymling" to tomatoes, spinach and beans. He was an up-to-date tiller of the earth, practicing crop rotation and contour plowing, and he railed against tobacco and other cash crops that exhausted the soil.

Carved right out of the hillside, the vegetable garden was supported by an 11-foot wall of uncemented stones. Many of the rough stones, some weighing half a ton and some small enough to be handled, were put to other uses after Jefferson's time. The wall was reassembled recently after students from the Monticello Field School of James Madison University and the University of Virginia excavated the original location.

The garden, orchard and vineyard were protected from pests by a ten-foot-high paling fence of chestnut boards, overlapped and narrowly spaced so "as not to let even a young hare in." Jefferson, ever the quantifier, estimated that it would take 300 posts, 900 rails and 7,500 boards to build the half-mile-long fence. Now, the restorers cannot wait to rebuild it, for baby rabbits and other creatures keep nibbling at the crops.

Smack in the middle of the garden Jefferson erected an observation-post pavilion that he called a "temple." It was an invigorating spot to sit, read and enjoy what he called his "sea view." Of that prospect on the east side of the little mountain, one of Jefferson's visitors wrote: "The eye is not checked by any object, since the mountain on which the house is seated commands all the neighboring heights as far as the

Chesapeake. The Atlantic might be seen, were it not for the greatness of the distance. . . ."

Like many of Jefferson's architectural creations, the garden pavilion idea was originally inspired by Palladio, the brilliant 16th-century Italian architect. Erected on the earth fill obtained for the garden by leveling the mountaintop, Jefferson's temple lasted only a short time, until a destructive storm knocked it down. Now it has been rebuilt on concrete foundations poured deep into the hillside. According to historian Beiswanger, the rebuilding of the pavilion has "established the presence of Jefferson in the garden, at the center of his horticultural world."

At one time, Jefferson thought about building several additional pavilions. Each of them would feature a distinctly different style of architecture, including, he noted, "a specimen of Chinese." But after drawing up a plan to locate the structures in the vegetable garden, he changed his mind. "[It] is not the place for ornaments of this kind," he explained. "Bowers and treillages suit that better, & these temples will be better disposed in the pleasure grounds." As far as anyone can tell, the original garden pavilion was the only one that was built.

The "pleasure grounds" Jefferson had in mind involved the creation of an 18-acre "grove" on the west side of Monticello. The woods there, he decreed, were to be "broken by clumps of thicket, as the open grounds of the English are broken by clumps of trees." He pruned and thinned the forest to obtain glades and vistas and envisioned a spiral arrangement of shrubs and "setting stone" seats beside cedar trees. Nearly two centuries after he drew up a plan for planting various trees and bushes in the grove, work began on a project to recreate it.

Just below Mulberry Row and his big garden, Jefferson laid out a vineyard and orchard. The trees, many of them peaches, no longer exist. With painstaking detective work and plenty of digging, however, the archaeologists have discovered old root stains that show where some of the original orchard trees and grapevine stood. "The soil is difficult to 'read' because it has so many hues of orange and red," Kelso says. "You can do it, but it takes experience." Presently, new trees are being planted in the old locations and in time the orchard will bloom and bear fruit once again.

Jefferson could never be accused of neglecting his vineyards or of being halfhearted about making wine. Over a period of years, he planted no fewer than 36 varieties of grapes. He was always hopeful that East Coast wines might someday replace those of France and Italy but, as it happened, his own production efforts were something less than sensational. Consequently, although he stored Virginia wine in the cellars of the main house, he usually ended up serving varieties that had been purchased overseas.

His collaborator in wine making was Philip Mazzei, an Italian with whom he would become close friends. Mazzei was a newcomer, looking for potential vineyard land, when a mutual friend brought him to Monticello. Immediately Mazzei became close to the affectionate and irresistible Jefferson. The master of Monticello soon gave to Mazzei a 193-acre parcel of land.

During his tours of Bordeaux, Burgundy and parts of Italy when he was Minister to France, Jefferson learned a great deal about European vineyards. Later, he applied that knowledge at Monticello. When Mazzei brought over a number of Italian vignerons to work in his own vineyards, two of them worked on Jefferson's, as well. Mazzei was one of many people with whom Jefferson exchanged seeds and plants, and when the Italian died in Pisa in 1816, his old friend keenly felt the loss.

Whatever in the world did Jefferson want with all of those fruit trees and grapevines and vegetables? Well, for one thing, he was an avid botanist and liked to experiment with seeds from all over the Eastern states, from Europe and from the Lewis and Clark expedition. For another, he was a generous host and family man. The 14 bedrooms at Monticello were often filled with children and guests who had to be fed.

Jefferson was a most persistent hunter-down of new seeds and plants. While he was Minister to France, for example, he took a three-week trip through the Piedmont rice lands of Italy. Though the penalty for exporting any of the Piedmont rice was death, he smuggled some grains out of Italy in his pockets.

Monticello horticulturist Peter Hatch has certainly had his work cut out for him by Jefferson. Thus far the ever-experimenting garden expert has located and planted hundreds of old varieties of fruit trees, vegetables and flowers; still to come are more than ten varieties of roses. Six of the trees that were living in Jefferson's time are still there: a sugar maple, two tulip poplars, a red cedar, a European larch and an American elm. Two of them had to be identified by boring into their trunks, extracting a cross section and counting the rings of annual growth. Hatch believes that about half of the fruit trees known to Jefferson are still obtainable, but many of the vegetables grown in those days are not. Soon he hopes to plant with the season of 1812 in mind; that was the year when Monticello's gardens were at their height of grandeur, and when Jefferson arranged his vegetables so that the root crops were all together, as were the leafy vegetables and the fruiting ones such as peas and beans.

Partly for the sake of his numerous grandchildren, Jefferson tried to avoid planting anything poisonous. In 1813 he turned down an offer from Dr. Samuel Brown, an amateur horticulturist, writing that "I have so many grandchildren and others who might be endangered by the poison plant, that I think the risk overbalances the curiosity of trying it. The most elegant thing of that kind known is a preparation of the Jamestown [jimson] weed, *Datura stramonium,* invented by the French in the time of Robespierre. Every man of firmness carried it constantly in his pocket to anticipate the guillotine. It brings on the sleep of death as quietly as fatigue does the ordinary sleep, without the least struggle or motion. . . ."

Visiting Monticello today, you feel at every moment the presence of the man who designed it. Jefferson liked to say the "the earth belongs to the living" and it almost seems as if he takes each visitor by the hand and proudly shows off what he has wrought. Strolling along the serpentine path among his flowers, or seeing the trim green lines of his spring-bright peas, or catching the magic of his sylvan glade, we know that Jefferson *loved* his garden. We can picture his hands curved in anticipation of fondling a full-blown peach, and we can think along with him as he records in his garden calendar the changes he is planning to make under the bright summer sun—knowing that he writes in the chill of a January rain.

In Monticello, we can sympathize with Jefferson's preference for the American climate, compared to what he had experienced abroad. As he told one friend in France, "I think it a more cheerful one. It is our cloudless sky which has eradicated from our constitutions all disposition to hang ourselves, which we might otherwise have inherited from our English ancestors."

We can imagine the master of his little mountain riding around almost daily, checking all of his ventures, always maintaining a cheerful view—even when the ventures turned into disasters. There was always next season, when this bush might be moved or that new seed could be tried or the vineyards might yield good wine—that eternal renewal of hope that every gardener who has ordered seeds from a catalog knows so well. Jefferson's joy in another gardener's successes, the seeds he kept sending to friends, speak so eloquently of his commitment that we gain a new insight into his character. His idea of the perfectibility of a house or a garden or a person becomes part of a whole. It is a gracious ideal and one he spent a full lifetime working to achieve, loving it all the way.

Richard L. Williams, "Atop a 'Little Mountain' in Virginia, Jefferson Cultivated His Botanical Bent," *Smithsonian* 15, no. 4 (1984): 68–77. Reprinted by permission.